T0328598

Cambridge Elements ≡

Elements in Creativity and Imagination
edited by
Anna Abraham
University of Georgia, USA

THERE'S NO SUCH THING AS CREATIVITY

How Plato and 20th Century Psychology Have Misled Us

John Baer
Rider University

CAMBRIDGE
UNIVERSITY PRESS

CAMBRIDGE
UNIVERSITY PRESS

University Printing House, Cambridge CB2 8BS, United Kingdom

One Liberty Plaza, 20th Floor, New York, NY 10006, USA

477 Williamstown Road, Port Melbourne, VIC 3207, Australia

314–321, 3rd Floor, Plot 3, Splendor Forum, Jasola District Centre, New Delhi – 110025, India

103 Penang Road, #05–06/07, Visioncrest Commercial, Singapore 238467

Cambridge University Press is part of the University of Cambridge.

It furthers the University's mission by disseminating knowledge in the pursuit of education, learning, and research at the highest international levels of excellence.

www.cambridge.org
Information on this title: www.cambridge.org/9781009073547
DOI: 10.1017/9781009064637

© John Baer 2022

First published 2022

A catalogue record for this publication is available from the British Library.

ISBN 978-1-009-07354-7 Paperback
ISSN 2752-3950 (online)
ISSN 2752-3942 (print)

There's No Such Thing as Creativity

How Plato and 20th Century Psychology Have Misled Us

Elements in Creativity and Imagination

DOI: 10.1017/9781009064637
First published online: June 2022

John Baer
Rider University
Author for correspondence: John Baer, baer@rider.edu

Abstract: Most people (including creativity researchers) act as if they believe that creativity is not simply a useful category or label but a real thing with its own essence (just as Plato would argue that an ideal triangle has an essence that is shared with all actual triangles). Most people (including creativity researchers) also believe that there is a set of general creativity-relevant skills that can be applied to most problems in ways that will lead to more creative outcomes. Creativity research now calls these beliefs into question. A domain-general misunderstanding of the nature of creativity-relevant skills and the equally mistaken belief that creativity exists independently of actual creative things and ideas have together hindered creativity theory, research, assessment, and training. A more domain-specific and nominalist understanding of creativity will free creativity researchers to make progress in areas where it is currently stymied.

Keywords: creativity, domain, domain specificity, domain generality, creativity theory

ISBNs: 9781009073547 (PB), 9781009064637 (OC)
ISSNs: 2752-3950 (online), 2752-3942 (print)

Contents

Introduction: Creativity Matters, so How We Think about It Matters

Is There a Creativity Crisis?

In July 2010 *Newsweek* magazine's cover announced that America was suffering a "Creativity Crisis." This was illustrated with a line-up of children's crayons arrayed like a plummeting graph. An ominous subheading spelled out the danger: "For the first time, research shows that American creativity is declining."

This is nonsense. As far as research can possibly determine such things – which is, I'm sad to report, not very far at all – there is not, and there was not in 2010, a crisis of any kind in American creativity.

The sensationalistic *Newsweek* cover was based on a reported twenty-year decline in scores on one very old test of creativity (Kim, 2011). Although once widely used, this is a test whose validity has been challenged for almost half a century.

Other measures of creativity, it turns out, show an *increase* in creativity over the same period of time that the supposed decline was happening (Gardner & Davis, 2013; Weinstein et al., 2014). But those results, which point in the opposite direction, are equally meaningless in regard to overall American creativity.

There is simply no way to know if creativity is waxing or waning in the USA as a whole. The question, as framed, has no possible answer, because there is no way to sum creativity in sculpture and creativity in cosmology, creativity in cooking and creativity in sports, creativity in interpersonal relations and creativity in poetry.

This contradiction – one set of creativity tests showing a decline, the other an upswing over the same period – is not surprising to anyone who knows much about what pass for "creativity tests." These tests routinely disagree with each other, even tests made and sold by the same test developers (including the one that showed the twenty-year decline). None of these tests can really tell us much about creativity *in general.*

So, in 2010 there was no reason, based on the research reported in the *Newsweek* story, to sell off one's portfolio of US stocks. (Disclaimer: Expertise – like creativity, as I will explain – is very domain specific. Being an expert in one domain does not make one an expert in other, unrelated domains. I've studied creativity for decades, have published scores of books and research papers about creativity, and have even won some awards for that work, so I can claim some expertise in this area. But I'm not an economist and have no expertise as a financial advisor. I know that there is no reason to believe there has been a general decline in American creativity, but I have no idea if there may have been other reasons to sell, or to buy, US securities back in 2010. Or at any other time.)

There is no creativity crisis, and yet there is a very real and important crisis in creativity. This crisis is not about tumbling scores on one (of many available) so-called "creativity tests," such as the one that the *Newsweek* magazine focused on. Nor is it about a sweeping, or even a slight, overall change in actual creative performance by either children or adults. There are changes over time, of course, but they are much more limited in scope. In some areas there is evidence for a modest increase, in others an similarly modest decrease (see, e.g., Gardner & Davis, 2013, and Weinstein et al., 2014, for examples of both increases and decreases in creativity over time in specific areas, and see Barbot & Said-Metwaly, 2021, for a more thorough explanation of where the research that was the basis for the *Newsweek* article went awry).

The crisis is in how we (mis)understand creativity – a misunderstanding that leads to poor creativity training and unreliable creativity assessment, both based on weak creativity theory and confused (and often contradictory) creativity research. It is the field of creativity *studies* that is in crisis, not actual creativity.

You may be breathing a sigh of relief and thinking, "So what? I care about actual creativity, not creativity research." And, in a way, you'd be right to think this. It's actual creativity we should care about. As long as their work doesn't impinge on actual creativity, what harm is there if creativity researchers and theorists (like me) are confused?

But creativity – whether in the form of monumental advances in science, or a toddler's epiphany; transcendent poetry, or a more tasty soufflé; solutions to world problems, or just a different way to complete the most mundane task – matters very much. Creativity matters for reasons ranging from the need to solve international problems that threaten the health of the planet to the simple joy that creativity, even creativity in small, pedestrian doses, brings to our lives. If we want to nurture creativity in children and adults – and a constant stream of books, TED talks, and opinion pages suggests that we do – we need better creativity theory and research.

In an interesting twist, *Newsweek*'s competitor *Time* also had a cover story about creativity, this one eleven years later. The schoolchildren whose alleged twenty-year decline in creativity that *Newsweek* reported in 2010 would thus be young adults at the time of *Time*'s June 28, 2021, cover story. These twenty- and thirty-year-old creative dullards, graduates of the "creativity crisis," were at just the right age in 2021 to bring that predicted crisis to a head in the real world. But the *Time* cover announced an "Innovation Boom," which is pretty much the opposite of a creativity crisis. "We're entering a new era of innovation," the story proclaimed. As it happened, the *Time* magazine story was about innovation in a specific domain – public health – not creativity in general. This, as we'll see, is exactly how we should be thinking about creativity, domain by domain. But that's getting ahead of our story.

Unusual Uses for a Brick

Unfortunately, most creativity theories (and the creativity research and creativity training based on those theories) are still stuck in Eisenhower-era models. Creativity research keeps de-bunking, and then modifying but essentially reinventing, the same theories, the same models, the same training, the same tests.

That creativity test that showed a twenty-year decline in scores? It was born in the 1950s. A half century ago, when the test was still relatively new, critics like University of California professor Susan Crockenberg were already arguing that the validity studies used to support that particular test (the Torrance Test of Creative Thinking) "should not be taken too seriously" (Crockenberg, 1972, p. 35).

A decade later a broader complaint emerged about the entire class of tests of which the *Newsweek* magazine test was just one example. These tests were (and are) all actually tests of divergent thinking, or DT. Some theorists have argued that DT may be part of creativity, but as Runco and Acar (2012) correctly note, DT test scores are, at best, possible "indicators of creative talent" (p. 66), not measures of creativity. DT tests are often mistakenly regarded as tests of creativity, however. Runco and Acar emphasize that this is "not a tenable view" (p. 67), and they are right, but the most widely used DT tests nonetheless call themselves tests of creativity, so it is not hard to understand how this confusion might have arisen. In the discussion that follows I will not test the reader's patience by continually making this distinction and will often refer to these tests as creativity tests, even though they are actually DT tests.

To understand the problem with DT tests as possible indicators or predictors of creativity one needs to understand what DT is. Fortunately, it's not a complicated idea. DT is simply the production of many different and unusual responses to an open-ended question. To qualify, the ideas needn't be good ideas. They just need to be original, and plentiful.

Coming up with lots of strange ideas, even totally unworkable, goofball ideas, surely *seems* like the kind of thing that should be related to creativity, doesn't it? The theory is indeed a compelling one.

About the same time DT was first proposed by Joy Guilford as a kind of thinking associated with creativity, and just before the first tests to measure it were created (whose direct descendant was the one cited in the *Newsweek* magazine "Creativity Crisis" story), Alex Osborn independently invented brainstorming as a way to produce a lot of it (DT, that is, even though that word wasn't yet available to describe it).

My students sometimes conflate DT and brainstorming, but brainstorming is just one tool for producing DT. It's like a shovel and a hole. We use a shovel to get a hole, but the two are very different things. Shovels are probably the most commonly used tool for making holes, and brainstorming the most commonly used tool for producing DT. But there are other ways to get both holes and DT. Just as we should not confuse shovels with holes, we need to distinguish the tool of brainstorming from the goal of DT.

Divergent-thinking tests pose tasks like making a list of interesting things one might do with a brick. Surely this requires creative thinking; as I said just a few paragraphs ago, the theory is a compelling one. The complaint? Divergent-thinking tests are fun, but they predict actual creativity – creativity in the arts, in the sciences, in problem-solving of all kinds – either poorly or not at all. They sometimes predict one kind of creativity but not others. DT of some kind may indeed be a component of some kinds of creative thinking, but the tests that have been designed to measure it simply don't tell us much about creativity in general.

How could that be? Here's an analogy: Spelling is a component of writing, but we wouldn't say that spelling tests are writing tests. There might be a positive correlation – better spellers might be better writers, although I know of no study that shows that, so that's just a guess – but surely such a spelling test wouldn't be a very good measure of writing skill in general. And what if the spelling test only included words related to a single topic, such as sports? A test that measured how well one could spell sports-related words would be even less valid as a test of writing. It might predict to some degree one's skill in writing about sports, but say nothing about one's ability to write about, say, biology or cooking.

These may seem like extreme cases, but in fact most DT tests don't measure DT in general, only DT in a particular domain. Even if they predict creativity (to a limited degree) in one domain – and it's not clear that they do, because researchers have too often been asking the wrong questions about DT tests, so we don't really know in which domains this might be true and in which it might not be – one thing is increasingly clear: They fail to predict creativity in unrelated domains.

American Psychological Association (APA) past-president Robert Sternberg summed up the emerging consensus four decades ago: DT tests, he argued, "capture, at best, only the most trivial aspects of creativity" (Sternberg, 1985, p. 618).

That opinion is widespread in the creativity research community today. As Sawyer put it in his popular creativity textbook, "most psychologists now agree that DT tests don't predict creative ability" (Sawyer, 2012, p. 51).

The continuing use of tests that most psychologists don't think are good predictors of creativity is why the APA sponsored a debate a few years ago on the question "Are the Torrance Tests Still Relevant in the 21st Century?" (The two Torrance Tests of Creative Thinking are the most widely used DT tests. One of them was the basis for the *Newsweek* magazine cover story.)

Note that the question that the APA asked was not along the lines of "How good are the tests?" or "When might they be useful?" but more on the order of "Are they any good at all?" and "Should they ever be used? (Full disclosure: I was the psychologist invited by the APA to argue for their nonrelevance. Probably not fair, then, for me to judge who "won" the debate. And as my counterpart in that debate is both a friend and a respected colleague, I wouldn't answer anyway. But I think it is fair to say that in being asked to argue that the Torrance Tests are irrelevant and should therefore be both mistrusted and avoided, I had the much easier assignment.)

So why are such tests still used? Because nothing better has come along, at least nothing better that is both cheap and easy to use. And even though we're not very good at measuring creativity – even though our efforts are mostly wasted, and even though we know that had we chosen a different creativity test we would likely have gotten totally different results (which should be a clear indication that our tests are invalid) – people nonetheless *want* to measure creativity. Almost desperately. After all, if something can't be measured, how can researchers study it? And what does it mean to describe something as increasing or decreasing, or even as present or absent, if it can't be measured?

With some trepidation, let me make a comparison to a very different kind of measure, IQ tests. IQ tests are very controversial (hence my apprehension in even mentioning them), and the validity of IQ tests is not a subject I want to broach. Except to say this: If the most widely used IQ tests were as varied in their results – if they disagreed with one another to the same extent – as the most widely used creativity tests, there would be no controversy about IQ test scores. None at all. Why not? Because no one would be using those IQ tests. And no one would think they were worth defending.

But creativity tests, as lame and as widely criticized as they are (and have long been), are still used, both in research and in identification for school programs. Why? Because creativity matters to us – as it should. So we want to find a way, we feel we *must* find a way, to measure it. We almost desperately want measures of creativity, because how else can we promote and research and even talk about creativity (or sell magazines proclaiming its decline)? But desperation is not the kind of motivation that typically leads to good decision-making.

I understand both the desire to measure creativity and the assumption that it must be measurable. Clearly some things are more creative than others, so it seems there must be some way to quantify those differences. But there is a real cost, and a real danger, in using such poor tests of creativity as the ones we have.

In computer science there's a saying, "Garbage in, garbage out." Nonsensical input data – or even just seriously flawed data that has at best marginal validity – produce nonsensical output. A different set of nonsensical or seriously flawed data would produce a different (equally nonsensical) result.

Sadly, one can prove almost anything one wants to prove about creativity simply by choosing the right test (and then someone else can *dis*prove the same thing by using a different test).

I don't mean to suggest that any creativity researchers – a group of people I respect greatly and am proud to count myself part of – are intentionally choosing tests that they know are either nonsensical or biased in order to falsely "prove" anything. But by unintentionally using tests of negligible validity – because that's pretty all that has been available – creativity researchers often, totally inadvertently, produce research findings that are very different from those one might find had a different test been used (as in the case of the "Creativity Crisis," where there are different measures of creativity that yield directly opposite results).

The problem is not with one test. Or with one theory, or one research program. If it were, psychological science would have replaced the bad tests, mistaken theories, and unproductive research programs with better ones. The problem is that creativity testing, creativity theory, and creativity research can't seem to find anything better. All are stuck, often recycling the same tired ideas year after year, decade after decade. It may not be quite so dire as Dietrich and Kanso (2010, p. 845) have argued: "Ideas first proposed in the 1960s and 1970s – laterality, divergent thinking, low arousal, remote associations, or defocused attention – are still those, and in essentially the same form, that drive current research efforts." It isn't really quite that bad. But almost.

Philosopher of science Thomas Kuhn argued that new paradigms only get widely accepted after those who held earlier views leave the field. Physicist Max Planck put it more bluntly: "A new scientific truth does not triumph by convincing its opponents and making them see the light, but rather because its opponents eventually die" (quoted in Kuhn, 1970, p. 151).

But the theorists, researchers, and test makers who developed what might be called the standard model of creativity in the 1950s and 1960s *have* left the stage. At least two generations of researchers and theorists later, the field remains stuck in the same ruts. It can't be the intransigence of long-gone leaders of the field that is causing the lack of progress.

Sometimes what a scientific field needs to replace is not its leaders. It needs to replace its assumptions. Here's an example: For centuries, scientists believed there was a luminiferous ether that allowed light waves to travel through empty space. Light was a wave, everyone agreed, and waves can't pass through a vacuum, so space could not be a vacuum. But it *is* a vacuum, and understanding light required letting go of a long-held belief in the ether. Similarly, the assumption that planetary orbits must be circular led to some very creative, and complicated, models of our solar system. Progress, however, required ditching that (seemingly obvious) assumption and working with *non*circular orbits.

Many smart and thoughtful people work in the field of creativity studies. Dedicated, curious, imaginative people who conduct ingenious studies designed to tease out creativity's mystery. It's not that we are learning nothing about creativity from their research. But they are hampered by an assumption about creativity that is simply false: the belief that creativity exists.

I hope you're thinking, "*Of course* creativity exists!" There are creative theories in science (and creative ways to test those theories). There are creative works of art of all kinds. There are creative recipes, creative songs, creative ways to resolve disputes with friends, creative ways to play with children, creative ways to coach sports teams, and even creative ways to conduct psychological research about creativity.

The list of things that can be done creatively is, happily, endless.

When I say that creativity doesn't exist, I should perhaps put scare quotes around it. The "creativity" that doesn't exist is the "creativity" that researchers and theorists – and the rest of us as well – typically assume is behind all the creative things and ideas we encounter. A creativity that exists apart from (and is at the same time a part of) actual creative things, ideas, and performances.

"Creativity" is typically taken to mean something that runs through and unifies all those creative things, some special feature (newness? originality? beauty?) that all creative things share. Alternatively, "creativity" is sometimes thought of as a special kind of thinking process, a way of approaching problems, habit of mind, motivation, or personality trait that *produces* all those creative things and ideas, something shared by creative people (and the rest of us, but to a lesser extent) that makes it possible to go beyond the obvious, the mundane, the routine. Either way – be it a unifying essence or a unifying process that produces that essence – creativity is thought of as something separate and distinct from actual creative things and ideas.

But that kind of "creativity" doesn't exist, even though there are, indeed, many creative things being produced every day, some world-altering, some hardly noticed. (There are also many creative thoughts, some of which may never even get expressed but are creative nonetheless.) What is false is the idea – the generally accepted idea, both inside and outside the creativity research community – that there is something in the world, something other than actual creative things or ideas, that corresponds to the word "creativity." And this false idea gets us into trouble.

Why This Matters

I used to be a creativity trainer. My classes lasted up to a week, and what I did – what I claimed I would do – was teach my students how to be more creative in anything and everything they did. I enjoyed those workshops, as did my students. I loved that I was making the world a better place by increasing the sum total of creativity and by making my students' lives better by increasing their individual creativity, which I believed (and continue to believe) is one of the things that makes life worth living.

But then, in 1983, Howard Gardner published *Frames of Mind*, in which he argued that there was no such thing as general intelligence. Domain-specific intelligences, yes – things like logical/mathematical intelligence, verbal intelligence, interpersonal intelligence, spatial intelligence – but each operated only in its domain. No general intelligence.

Psychologists for the most part disagreed. Of course there were specific abilities, whether in the domains Gardner had identified or in other domains. But there were also some general abilities that were applicable and useful pretty much across the board. Their chief method of demonstrating this general, domain-transcending ability or set of abilities was simple: They showed that there were substantial positive correlations in measures of performance across different domains.

As I wrote earlier, disputes about intelligence, or intelligence testing, are not my concern here. Whether you agree with Gardner about the nature of intelligence or agree with his critics makes little difference in terms of the reality of "creativity." But Gardner also suggested that creativity is likely to be domain specific in the same way, and although that was not the focus of his book, it was the part that I focused on because it challenged the possibility that the kind of creativity training I was doing was even possible. If all creativity was domain specific – if the thinking skills or ways to approach problems that led to creativity were different for every domain – then I had been selling my students a bill of goods. The kind of creativity I was teaching didn't exist.

There were many responses to Gardner's thesis, but the most compelling was the fact that if one measures abilities in a wide variety of domains, the people who exhibit more intelligence in one domain tend to do so for most domains. Put another way, there were large positive correlations on measures of ability – the kinds of abilities generally thought of as showing intelligence – across domains.

So what I needed to do was show that creativity worked that way too. That creativity in any one domain predicted creativity in other domains.

With a grant from the National Science Foundation, I set out to show this. At about the same time that Gardner's book came out, Teresa Amabile had developed a very powerful way to measure creativity that focused on creativity in specific domains. Unlike DT tests and other available measures of creativity, which generally assumed that creativity is domain general, her method – the Consensual Assessment Technique – didn't address the issue of domain specificity/generality at all, even implicitly.

The Consensual Assessment Technique was simply a way to assess creativity in a specific domain, and it could be used, at least theoretically, in any domain. How one interpreted the results of those tests was open. One could take them at face value as measures of creativity in the specific task and domain used in the assessment and therefore valid only as measures of creativity in that one domain. For example, if the task involved writing poetry, then the result could be interpreted as an indicator of poetry-writing creativity. If the task did not involve poetry but was, let's say, an art-related task, then it could be interpreted as an indicator of artistic creativity and say nothing, one way or the other, about poetry-writing creativity.

Alternatively, one could assume that the task used and the domain of that task didn't matter and that the creativity ratings based on any of these domain-based performances reflected creativity across the board, even though the task actually used in any of the assessments would necessarily come only from a single and very specific domain. Under such a domain-general interpretation, both a poetry-writing task and an art-creating task would actually be measuring the same thing: general creativity.

Amabile was interested in the effects of different kinds of motivation on creative performance. Addressing the specificity/generality question wasn't at all her goal in developing this approach to creativity assessment (the details of which we will consider below). She assumed that whatever one learned about, say, the effect of intrinsic versus extrinsic motivation on a person's creativity in collage-making would also be true of the effect of intrinsic versus extrinsic motivation on their creativity in other areas, like writing poetry. But because of the way her tests were designed, what she was actually measuring was creativity on a specific task, such as making collages, writing poetry, or writing stories (which were the three main tasks she used in her research).

Although not at all the purpose for which these tests were designed, they happened to be ideal for research on the domain-specificity/generality question. The appearance of this new method of creativity assessment just as as Gardner's unsettling book was published was perfect timing. (See Amabile, 1996, for a summary of the development of this approach to measuring creativity and the research she conducted with it. Unfortunately, the Consensual Assessment Technique is both very resource intensive and difficult to standardize, which often makes it difficult to use in many kinds of creativity research and in educational settings. See Baer, 2016, for a discussion of these issues.)

With Gardner's challenge in mind and Amabile's Consensual Assessment Technique in hand, I set out to show that creativity was highly domain general. Put another way, I expected to find that people who were highly creative when doing X were also more likely than chance to be creative when doing Y or Z.

What I found, however, in study after study, was exactly the opposite of what I had hoped to find. Creativity wasn't one thing; it was many, mostly unrelated things. More details about that initial research and the many follow-up studies that I and others conducted will come later. For now, let me be clear where we're going: I'm arguing that there is no such thing as "creativity" that exists apart from actual creative ideas, creative products, or creative performances. I'm claiming that those creative ideas, creative products, and creative performances are not produced by a similar set of thinking processes, problem-solving approaches, personality traits, or general skills, *and* that they do not share any essence or essential feature that makes them creative.

Philosophy: It All Goes Back to Plato

The claim that there is no such thing as creativity is related to an important idea in philosophy. Plato (everything goes back to Plato, doesn't it?) believed that there were individual things, like the mountain you plan to climb tomorrow, the courage with which you undertook some great challenge yesterday, and the chair you are sitting on today. No problem there. But Plato also believed there were things – ideal but very real things – that are the models for all actual, real-world mountains, instances of courage, and chairs, and it is these perfect models that give the less-than-perfect versions in which we encounter their essence.

Each mountain, each instance of courage, and each chair is independent and real, with particular features that distinguish it from other mountains, instances of courage, or chairs. But each (according to Plato) is based on a more universal, eternal, and unchanging *form*: an ideal and perfect mountain, an ideal conception of courage, an ideal chair. Everything in the world – every actual thing – is an imperfect version of a perfect form.

This idea, based on Plato's attempt to carve nature at its joints to discover its underlying structure and thereby reveal the nonphysical and perfect essences of all things, is called realism because it argues that general labels, labels that point to categories of things, refer to real things, things that are not simply convenient abstractions. Plato's forms are real; they exist not just because we decided to make category labels like chairs, mountains, and courage, or like justice, love, and beauty. So there is a true and perfect form for a chair, and all actual chairs participate in that form (but are not themselves perfect chairs). Ditto for beauty: All beautiful things participate, to varying degrees, in the true and perfect form of beauty.

Here's the part of this idea that may be hardest to wrap your mind around: Plato believed that those forms are not just words or ideas created by humans. They are not simply generalizations resulting from people's efforts to think about and understand what binds and unifies things that we think are similar. Nor are they merely produced by the wiring of our brains, by our innate proclivities to perceive the world in certain ways that evolution has found useful to adopt. The nature that Plato was carving at its joints is not the nature of the human mind. It is the nature, the true nature, of the world itself. Plato's forms have their own, independent reality. They exist apart from however we might happen to perceive them. They are separate from any actual instantiation of them, and they exist even if there are no observable instantiations of them – even if no examples of them could currently be found anywhere in the world. They are real in the deepest sense.

Plato argued that the material world is changeable and unreliable, but behind the unreliable world of appearances is a world of permanence. The forms exist whether or not any actual manifestations of those forms exist. "Creativity" could therefore exist, as an ideal form, even in the complete absence of any creative thing or thought.

Philosophy has a way of using certain terms in different ways, depending on context. There are, for example, multiple kinds of realism in philosophy. The position of realists who (like Plato) believe forms are real things is opposed not, in this case, by idealists, but by nominalists, who maintain that abstract concepts can exist and can often be useful without necessarily being real. Such abstractions can often be very powerful tools even though they do not exist except as humanly created generalizations. We have no reason to assume, nominalists argue, that a concept actually exists – that it is a part of the world, whether or not we humans happen to stumble across it – just because that concept, or the word we use to describe that concept, is in some way interesting to us or in some ways makes the world make sense to us.

This caution is obvious with some very unreal concepts like ghosts and unicorns, but it also applies to concepts that describe things that are very real to us. Consider, for example, beauty, love, justice, and luck. Is there something that exists in the world – not just in our heads, but out there in the real and permanent world – that corresponds to what we think of as "luck," a generalizable "luck" that is purely luck and nothing else, an eternal luck, a luck that is separable from any actual instance of luck? If humans had never invented the concept of luck – if humans or any similarly intelligent being had never evolved – would the category "luck" nonetheless have a real existence in the world, waiting to be discovered? How about beauty, love, and justice?

A Craving for Generality

Plato's love of general rules and of generalities of all kinds has shaped philosophy for more than two millennia, even while the term "forms" has faded. The search for "something in common to all the entities which we commonly subsume under a general term," which Wittgenstein referred to as a "craving for generality" (1965, p. 17), goes back to Plato (and probably much farther, but Plato was the first, as far as we know, to make this particular kind of craving explicit). Glennan (2017) traces this "craving" through the history of philosophy, right up to Wittgenstein's own work: "Wittgenstein's initial philosophical target is no doubt Plato and his theory of forms . . . [but] is by no means limited to Plato"; it can be seen through the history of philosophy "from Descartes's account of the nature of a body to Wittgenstein's own earlier attempts to characterize the general form of the proposition" (Glennan, 2017, p. 2). This "craving for generality" extends both broadly and deeply in philosophy. Wittgenstein's concern in some ways echoes Hume's uneasiness about what he viewed as an unwarranted commitment to a principle of the uniformity of nature.

Wittgenstein used the term "craving for generality" repeatedly in his lectures from the 1930s that became the *Blue and Brown Books* (1965) and suggested that this "method of reducing the explanation of natural phenomena to the smallest number of primitive natural laws" was a weakness that suffused the field of philosophy and was one of the chief sources of philosophical error, one that "leads the philosopher into complete darkness." Wittgenstein railed against this reductionistic tendency – one that characterized some of his own earlier work – as a "contemptuous attitude toward the particular case" (p. 18).

As an example of a critical weakness inherent in at least some forms of generalization, Wittgenstein famously argued that the term "game" has no core meaning. He pointed out that there was no shared feature, such as having rules, being competitive, requiring skill, or providing entertainment, that constituted a common element in all games (Wittgenstein, 1953). There are features shared by several or many games, but none that characterize games as a whole. There is no test that would allow one to say "This is a game, and that is not a game." Consider just ball games: "some, like tennis, have a complicated system of rules; but there is a game which consists just in throwing the ball as high as one can, or the game which children play of throwing a ball and running after it" (Kenny, 2008, p. 129).

The idea that a craving for generality has distorted our understanding in serious ways is not new. An interesting example is suggested in an early 18th-century argument for religious toleration. Bayle (1705), a favorite writer of Enlightenment scholars like Voltaire, Gibbon, Hume, Diderot, and Lessing, pointed out that people rarely act in accordance with their general moral principles:

> When one compares the morals of a religious man with the general idea one forms of that man's morals, one is astonished to find no conformity between the two things. The general idea supposes that a man who believes in a God, a paradise and a hell will do everything that he knows to be pleasing to God, and do nothing that he knows to be displeasing to Him. But that man's life shows us that he does exactly the opposite.
>
> (p. 9, as translated by Robertson, R. (2011). *The Enlightenment: The Pursuit of Happiness, 1680–1790*, HarperCollins, p. 117)

According to Bayle, moral principles give only general guidance, and neither that guidance nor those principles have any real effect on people's actions. Actual moral decisions are based solely on the details of particular situations. There are thus, Bayle goes on to argue, no grounds for believing that atheists would be any less moral in their actions than adherents to any particular faith. The interesting point in the current context, however, is simply Bayle's claim that general moral principles, even those that are loudly declaimed, are essentially empty insofar as they might influence specific moral decisions.

What Plato believed about forms – an idea that has influenced thinking, often indirectly, in more ways than it would be possible to catalogue here – implies that creativity has a reality all of its own, distinct from any specific creations, and that all creative things (be they works of art, dance routines, witty observations, scientific theories, game strategies, or whatever else might be judged creative) partake of this intrinsic quality. There is something, it is assumed, that binds all things creative, something that allows one to consider them a natural group: some quality that makes possible the study of this thing called "creativity" apart from any specific instantiations and without regard to discipline or provenance. But this is not, in fact, the case. There is actually very little if anything that creative things and ideas from diverse domains share. There is no communal essence that permeates the universe of creative things and ideas.

The idea that creativity is something – an essence, an augmentation, an inspiration – that all creative things, all creative people, and all creative ideas share to varying degrees is a fundamental misconception that leads people to act as if creativity were something conceptually distinct from, something in addition to, whatever thing or idea "creativity" is credited with animating: a supplement, a magical elixir, perhaps, that makes the ordinary extraordinary. Most people today (including creativity researchers) act as if they believe that creativity is not simply a useful category or label (as nominalists would argue) but a real thing with its own essence.

In contrast, consider a triangle, or just the idea of a triangle. One could argue that an ideal triangle has an essence that is shared with all actual triangles. But this is simply not true of all creative things, people, and ideas. This mistaken belief, although rarely expressed explicitly, provides the rationale for assuming that creativity is something one can study apart from its specific instantiations.

Fortunately, the larger form-matter debate needn't consume us. It may well be that some concepts exist in the world whether or not we identify or recognize them (such as number), while others may be totally human inventions (such as the rules of baseball). The only nominalist-realist question that matters here is whether creativity exists apart from any and all particular instances of actual thoughts, ideas, or things we might describe as "creative."

Would creativity exist even if no one had ever invented the term or the idea of "creativity"? If there were no humans to bestow the label "creative" on some things or ideas, would creativity exist? When we use the word "creativity," is there something that is shared by every creative scientific theory, every creative dance routine, every creative chess strategy, every creative painting, and every creative recipe?

The idea that all creative things and ideas share some essence is one definition, or perhaps I should say one sense, of what it means for something to be creative. Such a definition (or sense that there must be such a definition, whether or not it has actually been articulated) is the descendant, perhaps, of Plato's forms and his efforts to carve nature at its joints. We'll look at one such definition of creativity – sometimes called the standard definition – in the psychology section that follows. (Spoiler alert: It doesn't work.)

There is a second definition (or sense) of creativity that parallels this "longing for generality" approach to understanding creative things or performances, but with a focus not on the things created but instead on the *creator*, the person (or perhaps animal or machine) that produces creative things and ideas. This second (but related) approach assumes there must be something that gives birth to or shapes creative things, ideas, and performances – something that is the same thing whether it leads to a creative scientific theory, a creative dance routine, a creative chess strategy, a creative painting, or a creative recipe. It might be a thinking skill of some kind, a general approach to problem-solving, or a personality attribute. It could be a characteristic mental state of the creator, such as a willingness in whatever one does to "think outside the box." It could be an intrinsic motivational set that colors all of a person's interactions in the world, or just a general tolerance of ambiguity that leaves one open to all new, even poorly formed, ideas. Or it might merely be a set of work habits, or perhaps a technique one employs for producing DT such as brainstorming. It could, of course, be some combination of such things, with the stipulation that these combined skills, approaches, habits, etc., work to produce creative ideas, things, and performances no matter the kind of problem or goal. They lead to more creative ideas, performances, or creations across the board, wherever they are employed.

I'm going to argue that a general and meaningful definition that covers all creative things and ideas is not possible and that there is no set of skills or approaches that lead universally to more creative outcomes. That is what I mean in claiming that there is no such thing as creativity. I will show (a) why it matters that we recognize that "creativity" is an invented and very abstract concept that has little substance apart from each specific instance of creativity and (b) why it will make a huge difference in how we understand, nurture, and assess creativity if we free ourselves from this misunderstanding.

Reductionism has been a powerful tool in some arenas, such as physics. In others, the "craving for generality" that Wittgenstein decried has left us more in the dark. Creativity is one such arena.

(Two cautions: (1) There is some dispute about what Plato, and after him, Aristotle, meant by "forms." (2) I'm a psychologist, not a philosopher. There is much more to be said about Plato's forms. I will leave it to philosophers to say those things. Here, for example, is how the *Stanford Encyclopedia of Philosophy*[1] begins its discussion of Plato:

> Many people associate Plato with a few central doctrines that are advocated in his writings: The world that appears to our senses is in some way defective and filled with error, but there is a more real and perfect realm, populated by entities (called "forms" or "ideas") that are eternal, changeless, and in some sense paradigmatic for the structure and character of the world presented to our senses . . .. Nearly every major work of Plato is, in some way, devoted to or dependent on this distinction.)

---

[1] https://plato.stanford.edu/entries/plato/#DoePlaChaHisMinAboFor

Psychology: What Should Psychology Study?

Twentieth-Century Psychology Shares the Blame

Joy P. Guilford's 1950 Presidential Address has been widely and justifiably credited with bringing creativity into psychology's mainstream. Fifty years later, an entire issue of the *Creativity Research Journal* was dedicated to commemorating this speech.

Guilford did not view creativity as a single ability or trait (or anything along the lines of a Platonic form):

> [C]reativity represents patterns of primary abilities, patterns which can vary with different spheres of creative activity . . .. It is proposed that a fruitful exploratory approach to the domain of creativity is through a complete application of factor analysis, which would begin with carefully constructed hypotheses concerning the primary abilities and their properties. It is suggested that certain kinds of factors will be found, including sensitivity to problems, ideational fluency, flexibility of set, ideational novelty, synthesizing ability, analyzing ability, reorganizing or redefining ability, span of ideational structure, and evaluating ability. Each one of these hypotheses may be found to refer to more than one factor. (1950, p. 454)

His Structure of the Intellect Model (1967) pursued many of the factors that might contribute to creativity, but one part stood out: divergent production, which is sometimes called ideational fluency or (more commonly today) DT. Divergent production included twenty-four separate abilities that were hypothesized to be relatively independent not only of other intellectual abilities but of one another as well. Wallach and Kogan (1965) also produced tests of creativity, but "sought measures that, unlike Guilford's, would define a cohesive creative thinking dimension" (Richards, 1976, p. 152). Wallach (1970) claimed that the Wallach–Kogan measures defined a "unitary dimension" (p. 1251) of creativity, compared to the complex description of divergent production abilities put forward by Guilford.

The Guilford and Wallach–Kogan measures were soon dwarfed by yet another battery of DT tests, the Torrance Tests of Creative Thinking (the TTCT). Torrance actually created two very different tests, each with its own subtests, that measured different things. Both were (and are) considered tests of creative thinking, however, even though what they actually measure is DT skills in two different domains. It was one of the two Torrance Tests that led to *Newsweek* magazine's dramatic but misguided report of a "creativity crisis."

It is worth noting that Wallach later changed his mind about the value of DT tests, writing that "little if any of that systematic variation [in adult creative achievement] is captured by individual differences on ideational fluency tests"

(Wallach, 1976, p. 60). In other words, even one of the earliest architects of DT tests later determined that these tests (including the Torrance Tests, which were in wide use by the time Wallach did his about-face on the value of DT tests) had virtually no validity.

But there weren't any good alternatives to DT tests, and researchers needed some measure of creativity. A comprehensive survey conducted in 1984 reported that one of the two Torrance Tests had been used as a primary measure of creativity in roughly two-thirds of all published creativity research over the preceding ten years. The Torrance Tests dominated the field of creativity research to such an extent that, in what was intended as a comprehensive meta-analytic evaluation of the long-term effects of various creativity-training programs, only studies that used one of the Torrance Tests were included (Rose & Lin, 1984).

There are two Torrance Tests, the Verbal and Figural Forms. Both assess DT skills, but in different domains. Each produces multiple scores and indicators. Torrance apparently recognized both domain differences and other skill differences, more in line with the multifaceted and complex understanding of creativity that was the basis for the Guilford tests than the one-dimensional construct behind the Wallach–Kogan tests. In fact, Torrance was opposed to the use of composite scores. "Torrance has discouraged the use of composite scores for the TTCT. He warned that using a single score like a composite score may be misleading because each subscale score has an independent meaning" (Kim et al., 2006, p. 461). Torrance also never combined his two tests (Figural and Verbal) to produce a single overall score that in some way summed DT test scores in the two very different domains that his two tests focused on.

This is not how the tests have generally been used and interpreted, however. Contrary to Torrance's own advice, composite scores on his tests are widely reported and treated as measures of overall creativity, typically with no mention whatsoever of subscale scores. It is uncommon to find a creativity research study that looks at more than one of the two tests or that uses subscores or indicators rather than composite scores.

The writers of the *Newsweek* magazine "creativity crisis" story, like most other users of the Torrance Tests, ignored Torrance's advice and focused on just the overall score, exactly what Torrance had warned against.

The *Newsweek* story also claimed validation for the Torrance Tests based on a large study by Plucker (1999). This is an interesting claim, and one that *Newsweek* got wrong in a curious way. Plucker's widely cited study did indeed attempt to validate both Torrance Tests (Verbal and Figural), and Plucker was able to produce validation evidence supporting one – but only one – of the two Torrance Tests. There is much to say about the quality of that validation evidence, some of which I will say below, but even Plucker only claimed to have validated the Verbal Torrance Test. The data, he reported, did not support validation of the Figural Torrance Test; "figural DT was not a factor in the model" (p. 109) that predicted adult creative achievement. But it was in fact the Figural Torrance Test – the one that Plucker was not able to validate – that was the sole basis for the "creativity crisis" claim.

So Plucker had in fact failed to validate the Torrance Figural Test that was later the basis for the "creativity crisis" story. Sadly, this is not uncommon. Depending on how narrowly one defines creativity – depending, that is, on what limited criteria a study uses as its measure of actual creative performance – it is possible to "validate" many different tests, as long as one doesn't mind that the test will not predict creativity in most areas, just the one narrowly chosen. Plucker acknowledged this:

> The importance of verbal DT relative to figural DT may be due to a linguistic bias in the adult creative achievement checklists. For example, if a majority of the creative achievements required a high degree of linguistic talent, as opposed to spatial talent or problem solving talents, the verbal DT tests would be expected to have a significantly higher correlation to these types of achievement than other forms of DT. (1999, p. 110)

Plucker thus explained that the validation failure of the Torrance Figural Test and the validation success of the Verbal Test were the result of the criteria used in that study to define creativity. Those criteria – the "adult creative achievement checklists" that Plucker used as measures of actual adult creative performance – were essentially lists of self-reported creative accomplishments. The similarity between what the Torrance Verbal Test asked test takers to do (create extensive written lists in response to open-ended questions) and the later measure of adult creativity (which was based on self-reported lists of creative accomplishments) is striking. The two measures both rewarded making long lists of one kind or another, so whether or not such list-making had anything to do with creativity, one would expect subjects who were good at making long lists on one occasion might also make long lists on a later occasion.

But let's give the "adult creative achievement checklists" the benefit of the doubt. Let's posit that students who scored high on the Torrance Verbal Test were indeed more creative than those who scored lower on that test (at least on tasks that "required a high degree of linguistic talent"). What is significant in Plucker's analysis is that students who scored high on the *other* kinds of DT questions (the ones from the Figural Test, which did not ask test takers to make lists) were apparently *not* more creative than those who scored lower on the same Figural Test, at least not enough to make it part of the model Plucker was able to create linking the tests with later creative achievement.

Other tests, Plucker indicated, might measure creativity in other areas such as "spatial talent or problem solving talents." Different kinds of creativity would require different tests, it seemed. The Torrance Figural Test might be such a test; even though it was of little help predicting creativity that involved linguistic skills, it might predict other kinds of creativity. It *might*. Or it might *not*. We simply don't know, based on Plucker's study, what kinds of creativity, if any, the Torrance Figural Test can predict.

Plucker's validation effort thus seems to undercut any claim that the Torrance Tests are measuring creativity in general. The two tests appear, at best, to be measuring two different kinds of creativity. But if each creativity test measures a different kind of creativity, and if every kind of creativity requires its own, specialized test, then there's no such thing as *general* creativity, is there? Plucker's validation study showed the Torrance Tests are, at best, measures of creativity in limited domains – a conclusion that could only support a domain-specific understanding of creativity.

A decade after Plucker's study, Runco et al. (2010) reported the results of a fifty-year longitudinal study designed to assess the validity of the verbal form of the Torrance Test of Creativity. Like Plucker, Runco et al. were in fact able to provide evidence that supported the validity of this test as an indicator of *some kinds* of creativity, but not of other kinds of creativity. Evidence, that is, that the test was valid as a domain-specific indicator of possible creative achievement but not as a domain-general indicator of creativity.

Runco et al. reported that "TTCT scores were moderately correlated with personal, but not with public, achievement" (p. 361). Both public and personal achievement were assessed by self-report. Public achievement includes the kinds of things one would normally think of as achievements, whereas personal achievements are "activities and experiences that are not always socially recognized" (p. 362):

> Participants were asked to respond to questions about everyday creative behavior, including things such as having organized an action-group (food cooperative, environmental pressure group, etc.), designed a house, started a new school or other educational program, had a striking religious experience, or become seriously involved in a new hobby. (p. 362)

These are indeed achievements that show activity and engagement. Are they creative achievements? That is certainly arguable, but this isn't the place to debate whether things like self-reported involvement in a new hobby are appropriate measures of creative achievement. For our purposes we can simply accept the findings as reported. What is notable in the context of the domain-specificity issue is that the TTCT predicted only some limited kinds of creativity. It did *not* predict the kinds of achievements more typically thought of as creative achievements, the ones the authors describe as public achievement.

Runco et al. advance a curious possible explanation for the failure of the TTCT to predict public achievement:

> It may be that participants are now at a stage of life where personal achievements are more important than public ones. (p. 366)

If the participants were mostly long-retired nonagenarians, this might make sense, but "[t]he average age of the participants is 56 years" (p. 363), a time of life when people tend to be at the most productive period of their careers. This is certainly not a time of life when public achievement is no longer of interest to most people.

There is a much simpler explanation: *The DT that the TTCT measures is only an indicator of achievement in some domains but not others.* Like the Plucker (1999) validation study, this longitudinal study appears to be providing evidence that the predictions of this fifty-year-old DT test are domain specific. The test does appear to predict creativity in at least one domain, but not in others.

And yet the Torrance Tests and the domain-generality assumption are still with us. Plucker (1999) noted that "DT tests have recently fallen out of favor [and] critics have pointed out that the Torrance Tests of Creative Thinking ... are fraught with methodological weaknesses" (p. 111). But both of the Torrance Tests continue to be used. There still aren't any good alternatives for large-scale and inexpensive creativity testing, the kind needed in many research studies, and the Torrance Tests, though fallen out of favor, are still available. It is perhaps for this reason, together with the domain-generality assumption and the perceived need for some kind of creativity test, that the message from Plucker's validation study and the Runco et al. (2010) longitudinal study has sometimes been interpreted – *mis*interpreted – as suggesting that the Torrance Tests have been validated as measures of creativity. Which is what the *Newsweek* study did, despite the fact that these studies have provided only very limited and domain-specific support for the validity of the TTCT.

Boring (1923) famously made the tautological claim that intelligence is whatever intelligence tests measure. Setting aside any question about the validity or value of IQ tests, in at least one sense this assertion is undeniably true: What people will think of as intelligence will be shaped by whatever it is that is measured in IQ tests.

So it is, and has been, with creativity. I do not mean to suggest that Guilford's Structure of the Intellect model was correct or that the tests he developed of different aspects of DT were on the right (or wrong) track. But because single-dimensional creativity tests scores have ruled psychology for a half century – the Torrance Tests alone were the measure used in two-thirds of creativity studies over an extended period, as reported above, and most of the other measures of creativity used during that period also supported a one-dimensional conception of creativity – it should come as no surprise that single-dimensional conceptions of creativity are what guide both folk psychology understandings of creativity and much of the work done by creativity researchers. Operational definitions define a construct, and operational definitions of creativity have, for the most part, supported the "craving for generality" notion of what creativity is.

I have been focusing on two ways of thinking about creativity, going back and forth between the two perhaps too freely without acknowledging their difference. Psychologists call these "process" and "product" conceptions of creativity. A creative process is a way of thinking about, approaching, or solving problems that leads to (but is not at all the same as) actual creative things and ideas. The DT model is a prime example of this process approach to conceptualizing creativity. A creative product understanding of creativity, in contrast, is based on actual creative things and ideas, not how they came into existence. In this focus on what is created (and not the thinking, skills, or goals of the person that were needed to bring forth the created product), a product-based understanding of creativity is in line with a "craving for generality" theory that assumes all creative things share some essential similarities, some shared essence.

Although they do so in different ways, both the process and product approaches generally presuppose that creativity transcends individual creative efforts or domains of creativity and that there is a oneness to creativity despite its very diverse instantiations.

There are two other common conceptions of creativity. One of these focuses on the *person* who creates, the other on the *environment* that elicits and judges creativity. For the purposes of this discussion, the "person" definition can be folded easily into "process" (or vice versa); the process is carried out by a person, and a person's skills and personality traits matter because of what they cause the person to do. This is not to deny that the distinction between person and process views is a useful one, only that it is not needed in this context.

As for the environment (which often goes by the label "press" so that this can be called the 4-P model), one can acknowledge the effects of environments (as I do) without claiming that creativity actually resides there, so I will mostly ignore it.

What Should Psychology Study?

Think for a moment about what it means for something or someone to be "good." There are many things to which we apply the adjective "good." A theory can be good, a joke can be good, a parking spot can be good, a dinner can be good, luck can be good, a poem can be good, and just about any behavior can be good (unless it's bad, of course, or just so-so). The list of things people are or do that might be described as "good" is endless; we use the word all the time. Teachers tell students that something they have done or said is "good" so often that psychologists worry about possible negative consequences of overusing such simple praise.

Goodness is clearly something that matters to us a great deal. We describe both people and the things they do as "good" every day. It's something we think about constantly ("Did she do a good job?," "Did your lecture draw a good crowd?," "Did the golfer hit a good shot?," "Does the room need a good cleaning?," "Will I make a good impression?").

What "good" means depends on the context in which we use it, so much so that the same thing can be simultaneously both good and bad. For example: "It was a good joke, but a bad way to start his speech," or "It tastes so good, but is so bad for my health!" Goodness matters to us, but we don't think the quality of being good has some internal coherence, nor do we assume that there is some set of skills that lead to good performance no matter the domain or context.

Imagine a psychology of goodness. Goodness research would certainly stumble due to the wide variety of meanings that "goodness" encompasses. One study might show that goodness is correlated with trait X, whereas other studies might find that goodness is correlated with the *opposite* of trait X. For example, good salespeople might be found to have a high degree of extraversion, whereas good truck drivers might be found to have low degrees of extraversion. Even in the same domain, what makes something good or bad might depend on the specific context (e.g., in tennis good serves might be correlated with hitting the ball harder, but this would not be the case with good drop shots). As a result, the correlations researchers might find between traits, abilities, performances, products, etc., on the one hand, and goodness, on the other, would depend on the particular population, context, or some other variable.

There is nothing incompatible about extraversion being correlated with one kind of goodness and introversion being compatible with other kinds of goodness – *unless* we were foolish and tried to study goodness as a generic construct. Such a field of study would inevitably be rife with conflicting research findings, pointless debates, and little progress.

Fortunately, all of us have the good sense (Hmmm – What does "good" mean here?) not to expect a great deal of consistency in what we mean when we describe something as "good." And so we don't have pointless disputes of this kind (e.g., "Extraversion leads to goodness, so we should cultivate extraversion!" versus "Introversion leads to goodness, so we should cultivate introversion!"). But that is true only because we recognize that different understandings of what goodness means are incompatible. Trying to see goodness as a general attribute could get us quickly into trouble.

Does the fact that we don't (and shouldn't) study "goodness" as an abstract quality mean that we don't (and can't) understand goodness in its many diverse manifestations? Not at all. We can understand (and if we wish, study) what makes a dance routine (or a computer programming subroutine) good; what makes a boxing match (or a box of matches) good; or what makes a wedding toast (or cinnamon toast) good. But studying these different kinds of goodness as if goodness were a single thing – assuming that because they all involve "goodness" they must have an important underlying unity – would make it much harder to understand any of them very well. It would distort our understanding of them and lead to confusion, not to clarity or comprehension.

It seems that the wide varieties of things people approve of might vary too much to make a study of "goodness" profitable. The fact that people generally approve of sunny weather, conventional manners, and a low price doesn't mean they share any significant characteristic or cause, even though we call them all "good." This doesn't mean we should avoid using the term, of course, or that we should not try to do good things. In specific contexts, we generally understand what we mean by "good." But those meanings vary enormously across contexts. Lumping them together to study what it might mean to be "good" would necessarily obscure those important differences and focus on whatever (probably inconsequential) similarity they all share. Deciding not to study the psychology of goodness is merely a recognition that even though we care a great deal about goodness and know what we mean when we use the term, a psychology of goodness might not be a wise road to travel.

In *Principia Ethica,* Moore & Baldwin (1993) declared the "good is indefinable" (p. 9); as Kwame Anthony Appiah (who writes "The Ethicist" column for the *New York Times*) observed in *Experiments in Ethics* (2008):

> Goodness seems to be plural: *there's no such thing as goodness in itself.* [To be good] is always to be good in a way. We can parse these various ways of being good, see the virtues as admirable in distinctive ways and for distinctive reason. (p. 68; italics added for emphasis)

There is no essence, no core, no fundamental quality, or set of defining features that define what it means to be good. This is precisely the argument I am making about creativity: There is no such thing as creativity in itself.

Creativity as an Abstraction

Creative thinking (whether by a genius or a child, whether thinking about art or science or how better to upholster a sofa) is generally thought of as a *kind* of thinking. It is a kind of thinking that at least sometimes produces something (an idea, product, or performance) that we think is creative. The term "creative thinking" doesn't refer only to a particular instance of creative thought. It refers to creative thinking in general.

And if creative ideas, products, or performances are in some way alike; if creativity exists apart from individual examples of creative ideas, products, or performances; if the term "creativity" has any meaning that is independent of particular instances of creative ideas, products, or performances – then they must share something, some essential element, spirit, or feature that results in their being more creative than other things.

So "creativity" is (a) a kind of thinking or (b) an important aspect, feature, essence, or component of all ideas, products, or performances that we deem creative. Either way, it's a term that implies there is something similar in the things it refers to, something shared by those things.

"Creativity," as the word is commonly used, is an abstraction.

Abstractions can be powerful when used wisely. But abstractions can also be misleading. Gramsci (2011) once wrote that "'One equals one' is an abstraction, but nobody is led to think that one fly equals one elephant" (p. 230). Numbers – perhaps the best example of true Platonic forms – are abstractions. The number three can be thought to exist entirely independently of the existence of any particular trio of things.

Even granting "three-ness" a reality, however – a perfect three-ness of which any trio of things is an example – does not make things that come in threes more like one another in any other respect. For the most part, what three poems, three bridges, three dance routines, three theories, and three computer programs have in common – three-ness – is a very trivial connection.

In the same way, even if creativity were a true Platonic form even if all creative things shared a creative essence, just as all collections of three things share in having an essential three-ness as a way one might describe them – that shared creative essence might have little meaning or significance. A creative poem, a creative bridge, a creative dance routine, a creative theory, and a creative computer program might still be like one another in only the most trivial way. In fact, this is true of of the standard definition of creativity used by psychologists.

To the extent that creativity researchers and theorists are able to define creativity, they say that to be creative something must be new (original) and appropriate to the situation or constraints. Just being strange isn't enough; a creative product must indeed be strange (in the sense of being novel), but it must also work.

Fair enough, but this is not a very useful definition, and not really what people tend to think about when judging whether a poem, a painting, or a play is creative. What does it mean for a poem, a painting, or a play to work? *Leaves of Grass,* The Last Supper, and *Love's Labors Lost* are all original, and they all work, but they have about as much in common as three elephants, three planets, and three consonants. Or, to make the point a slightly different way, the Taj Mahal, standard copy paper, and sugar are all white, but their shared whiteness doesn't make them similar in any significant way or tell us much about any of them.[2]

Twenty dandelions share many features, so saying that something is a dandelion tells us quite a lot about it. But even though a dandelion may share the yellow color of a yellow crayon, a yellow tomato, and a yellow

---

[2] Shakespeare made this point in yet another way in Sonnet 130:

> My mistress' eyes are nothing like the sun;
> Coral is far more red than her lips' red;
> If snow be white, why then her breasts are dun;
> If hairs be wires, black wires grow on her head.
> I have seen roses damasked, red and white,
> But no such roses see I in her cheeks;
> And in some perfumes is there more delight
> Than in the breath that from my mistress reeks.
> I love to hear her speak, yet well I know
> That music hath a far more pleasing sound;
> I grant I never saw a goddess go;
> My mistress, when she walks, treads on the ground.
>   And yet, by heaven, I think my love as rare
>   As any she belied with false compare.

Yes, there are similarities, but the red of coral and the red of her lips differ in intensity (and perhaps other ways) such that pointing out their shared redness isn't helpful in describing her. In the same way, many things may also be fairly deemed creative (some, of course, more creative than others), but the shared quality of being creative is unhelpful because different creative things are (almost by definition) not at all the same, and lumping them together as "creative" tells us little about the actual things described as creative. Pointing to the fact that they are both original and appropriate to their particular situations of contexts – which is all the standard definition of creativity tells us – adds little to our understanding of them.

school bus, saying the dandelion is yellow doesn't connect it in a significant way with the crayon, tomato, school bus, or any other yellow thing, and linking the four provides only a very thin description of any of them. Yes, one can argue that yellowness exists, and perhaps in a way that can be defined much more effectively than creativity, but for most yellow things, it is far from definitive. The far more indeterminate original-and-appropriate definition of creativity is so thin that it tells us almost nothing about what makes a poem, a painting, or a play interesting. Saying something is original and that it works in a given context says little more than saying that it's creative. So the standard definition tells us that something is creative if it's creative. That clarifies things.

And what thinking skills or processes let to the creation of *Leaves of Grass,* The Last Supper, and *Love's Labors Lost?* Were they they same, or even similar?

Whether one wants to focus on creative things, creative people, creative ideas, or creative ways of thinking or acting, there is simply no fundamental quality or set of defining features that define what it means to be creative. There is no such thing as creativity in itself.

Let's look at another abstraction that both psychology and commonsense have adopted a much more suitable way to think about.

The Case of Expertise

The idea of studying the nature of goodness and what "good" means might seem a little extreme, which is why I chose it as an example. Now let's try a far less extreme example, this time of a concept that is, like creativity, actually studied by psychologists: "expertise." The concept of expertise has an intuitively appealing uniformity of meaning. When we think of what it means to be an expert, we mean that the person knows a lot about something or has a great deal of skill doing something. Expertise is skill in doing something or knowledge about something.

Our definition of creativity – things or ideas that are new and appropriate to the situation – worked in the sense that it seemed to include all kinds of creativity, but it didn't really tell us much about what creativity actually is. How well does "skill in doing something or knowledge about something" work as a definition of expertise?

There does seem to be an underlying unity to the concept of expertise. But as with creativity, that unity is largely illusory. A slightly different definition points out the problem: Expertise is skill or knowledge *in a particular domain.* Although we call them all by the same name, expertise in different domains –

what it means to be an expert in each domain – may actually have absolutely no overlap at all.

Consider the domains of differential calculus, California wines, Japanese cinema, auto repair, reading X-rays, throwing pots, and pitching curve balls. If we did Venn diagrams of what counts as expertise in each, we'd have seven circles that don't even touch each other. One could add domain after domain – map-making, two-handed backhands, Early Renaissance art, neurology, diagramming sentences, Hadrian's Wall, tap dancing . . .. Each kind of expertise is its own domain of skills and knowledge. It's possible to name domains in which expertise probably does overlap somewhat (e.g., tap dancing and drumming). But make a list of 100 kinds of expertise and randomly pair them and you're likely to find zero overlap in what constitutes expertise in most of the pairs.

There is one thing most kinds of expertise have in common: The acquisition of expertise in most domains requires practice, study, and feedback of some kind over an extended period of time. But study and practice are no more part of the content of expertise than a shovel is part of a hole. One may use a shovel to get a hole, just as one may need practice to acquire expertise. But shovels are not part of holes, and neither are study and practice part of expertise. Nor does having the former mean you have or can get the latter. You can have a shovel but no hole (maybe the ground is just too hard, or you're not strong enough), and you can practice a lot without acquiring expertise. (My tennis game is a perfect example of this.)

There's really not much one can say about expertise in general, except this: Expertise is highly domain specific. Which is precisely why there isn't much one can say about expertise in general.

It's possible to learn a great deal about what it means to be an expert in a given domain, but knowing what it means to be an expert in one domain, such as suspension bridges, is unlikely to tell us what it means to be an expert in most other domains, such as the bones of the upper part of the nose, the periodic table, silent movies, or catalytic converters. And conducting research about the particular skills, knowledge, personality traits, dispositions, environments, or other factors that lead to or promote expertise in one domain will tell us little about what skills, personality traits, dispositions, environments, or other factors lead to or promote expertise in other domains. Other than the simple fact that they are all likely to take a considerable amount of time, the things that lead to expertise in map-making, two-handed backhands, French Renaissance art, neurology, diagramming sentences, Hadrian's Wall, and tap dancing are likely to be quite different. (And not all expertise even requires long periods of study or practice. One can, for example, become an expert in the rules of tic-tac-toe both quickly and easily.)

Are you thinking that working hard and perseverance are common personality traits among experts? They certainly seem to be. But many people work hard and persevere without becoming experts. (Need I mention my tennis game again?) There is also a degree of domain specificity to hard work and perseverance. One may be willing to work hard and persevere in some domains (such as reading X-rays and practicing a two-handed backhand), but not at all in others (such as reading the Talmud or practicing juggling). I'll grant that hard work and perseverance are traits that many experts have. But does that tell us much about expertise?

In considering creativity, we asked (a) if all creative things and ideas had some shared essence or (b) if there were a shared set of skills or traits that tended to produce creative things and ideas. There are two parallel ways we might try to understand expertise, either in terms of the content needed to be an expert or in terms of the skills needed to acquire or demonstrate expertise. About content: Is there much overlap in what it means to be an expert in reading X-rays or in juggling? About skills: Can I take the same abilities that I relied on in learning to juggle and use them to learn to read X-rays? I think not.

This is why there could be no meaningful test of expertise in general. One could certainly assess levels of expertise in map-making, two-handed backhands, French Renaissance art, neurology, diagramming sentences, Hadrian's Wall, and tap dancing (okay, that's the last time for that particular list). But a test for expertise *in general,* a test that would give an estimate of someone's proficiency in all those domains (and all the other domains one might add to the list)? Impossible. Trying to create such a test would be a fool's errand, and only fools would pay attention to any scores it produced.

For the same reason – the domain specificity of expertise – no one would assume that by studying expertise in map-making one would learn much about what expertise is like in surfing, or what expertise is like in general. Different domains, different sets of skills and knowledge.

And yet that's how most of us tend to think about creativity, as if creativity were fungible, like money, which can be spent pretty much anywhere to buy just about anything. Money may not buy love, as the Beatles reminded us, but it can buy an incredibly diverse array of things; one doesn't need different kinds of money to buy food, books, software, health care, toys, concert tickets, gardening tools, or bicycles. But creativity doesn't work that way. It isn't some readily transferable skill or quality that one can simply take from domain to domain. No one would assume that to be true of expertise. (Can you please apply your expertise in Japanese cinema to interpret this set of tree rings for me?) Nor would we assume that because someone is an expert in diagramming sentences that they will probably know something about auto repair.

Why do so readily we make this kind of assumption with creativity?

Domain Specificity of Creativity

Albert Einstein, Emily Dickinson, Pablo Picasso, Zora Neale Hurston, Yasunari Kawabata, Martha Graham, Steve Jobs, Murasaki Shikibu, Marie Curie, Katsushika Hokusai, Simone de Beauvoir: How are they alike? Beyond the respect with which we bequeath the accolade "creative" to them, what similarities are there in their personalities, their thought processes, their motivations, their backgrounds, their environments, or what they created? They were all geniuses, of course, and they all contributed to their respective fields, but this is like saying they were all experts (or that they were all very good at something). It tells us nothing about who they were or what they did. Expertise, goodness, creativity: All are domain specific.

One could, perhaps, say that they were all highly motivated, but so are many people who achieve much less. And motivation isn't interchangeable across tasks or activities. I can't transfer my motivation to play guitar to motivation to sculpt, or my motivation to solve word puzzles to motivation to grade papers. (Sometimes my motivation to *avoid* grading papers turns into motivation to do other things, but that's different.) Even if we assume that each genius in my list was highly motivated to do *something,* the things they were motivated to do are incredibly diverse. Saying they are similar because each was highly motivated is rather like saying a gallon container of poison, a gallon container of beer, and a gallon container of sand are alike in some special way – and that each is unlike a quart or pint container of poison, beer, or sand. Although the size of the container matters, in most contexts its content matters much more.

Although these creative geniuses were all presumably motivated to do amazing things (their motivation would certainly be measured in gallons, not pints or quarts), the motivational content of each – what it was they aspired to do, and what it was they actually did – could hardly be more diverse. Each of the creators in my list had a strong desire to do something, but what each wanted to do was quite different from what the others wanted to do. Their motivation was, in each case, fairly specific.

Emily Dickinson was highly motivated to write poems, not to dance or write novels or paint. Motivation isn't fungible, able to be transmuted into whatever kind of motivation might be wanted at the moment. It is domain specific. (Important clarification: It is certainly true that some people are motivated in lots of areas, others in few. But even people who are motivated in many areas are not simply motivated in general; they don't find *everything* equally interesting or worth devoting their time to. There are people who are motivated to become mayor of their town, or to remove leaves from gutters, or to climb mountains.

But not the people in my list of geniuses above, who showed no special interest in any of these things.)

Domain specificity doesn't mean a person can only be motivated, or creative, in a single domain. It simply means that motivation and creativity depend on domain, and that knowing someone is motivated – or creative – in one domain does not imply that they are motivated – or creative – in all or even most other domains. The same can be said of many other traits commonly associated with creativity, such as openness to experience. I'm very open to new experiences in some domains, but not in others (e.g., fire eating, rodeo riding, or tightrope walking).

So geniuses tend to be highly motivated, but surely the world is filled with highly motivated people who do not strike us as creative geniuses. I know many teachers, musicians, and scholars who are highly motivated – some of them obsessively so – who are not especially creative in their work. (They may be creative in other areas, however: a highly motivated but dull teacher might nonetheless be a creative musician or wood-worker or writer; an ambitious but uninspiring musician might in her off-hours be a creative scholar or chef or teacher; and a hard-working but unstimulating scholar might surprise his colleagues if they learned what a creative dancer, soccer coach, or gardener he happened to be.) Although it's certainly possible to be highly creative in any of those domains, many highly motivated people in those fields – many highly motivated people in almost *any* domain – are not particularly creative.

So even if we could agree that these extraordinarily creative people were highly motivated, that doesn't make them all that unusual. High levels of motivation may be necessary for creativity at the highest levels in most domains, but most highly motivated people aren't creative geniuses. And like creative geniuses, the motivation of us mere mortals is also very domain specific.

There is even evidence that too much of some kinds of motivation (such as extrinsic motivation focused on doing something to earn a reward or a positive evaluation) may sometimes impede creativity (Amabile, 1996; but it's complicated, and even here the answer is often "It depends"; see, e.g., Cameron & Pierce, 1994, and Eisenberger & Shanock, 2003).

Albert Einstein, Emily Dickinson, Pablo Picasso, Zora Neale Hurston, Yasunari Kawabata, Martha Graham, Steve Jobs, Murasaki Shikibu, Marie Curie, Katsushika Hokusai, and Simone de Beauvoir were all immensely creative. Surely their similarities should tell us something – should tell us a *lot* – about what creativity is. And yet it is hard to find just exactly what it is they had in common, or what their diverse creations have in common. What is the essence of the "creativity" that they or their creations shared? The closer one looks, the more it seems that essence, that *sine qua non* of creativity, simply doesn't exist.

Each creative genius exhibits a way of thinking in their respective domain beyond the typical or expected, a way of taking a different perspective, of seeing things others cannot. But is this in any way a *shared* way of thinking, a cognitive process or problem-solving approach that they all used but that less creative people don't or can't use (or can't use to the same degree)? And whatever the source of their creativity, might each have deployed that magic as successfully in some other field? Could Einstein, who loved music, have been a great composer? Could he have been a great novelist? Picasso wrote a great deal of poetry, but would anyone be reading his poems today if he had not been an artistic genius? Might he have been a brilliantly creative astronomer had he tried? Dickinson had an extensive herbarium and gathered, grew, and classified many kinds of flowers, but had she applied her creativity to botany instead of poetry, would she be famous today? Might she have instead been a great composer?

Is it possible to apply one's creativity in any domain, or are the things that make one's creativity-relevant skills and traits domain specific?

Consider for a moment your own creativity, and that of people you know. You may be creative in several areas or just a few (I'm sure the readers of this treatise are likely to skew in the "creative in several areas" direction!), but the crucial question is this: Could you take whatever it is that makes you a creative chef, a creative poet, a creative teacher, or a creative dancer, and apply that creativity in domains in which you are currently not very creative?

Most of us do many things and have familiarity with multiple domains, and yet we are much more creative in some areas than we are in others. If creativity were a general skill, trait, or disposition, we should be able to apply it anywhere. If someone is a fast runner, that will transfer from sport to sport; a fast sprinter will be at an advantage, other things being equal, in many sports. But creativity doesn't work that way. One person might be a creative poet and a creative sculptor, but not at all creative when teaching; another person might be a creative teacher and a creative sculptor, but try as she might finds herself unable to do much with poetry; and others might be creative in all three areas, or in just one or none of the three. (Creativity is not dichotomous, of course. It's not that simple: People aren't either creative or not creative. In almost any domain, levels of creative performance fall on a continuum, with an infinite range of more and less creative.)

Creativity in one domain doesn't predict creativity in other domains. There is a lot of research evidence to back this up, but for now, just think about your own creativity, and that of people you know. Creativity is just like expertise, is it not?

One person might have expertise in auto mechanics and classical music, but not in poetry or math, while someone else might be an expert in all four areas, in none of the four, or in any mix of the four. Creativity works the same way. Some people are highly creative in many domains and some in just a few (or none), but on the whole, creativity in any one domain doesn't predict creativity in any other domain (unless the two are closely related, of course; a creative painter might be more likely than chance to be creative in drawing or making collages).

But what about polymaths like Leonardo da Vinci, people who were exceedingly creative in multiple domains? Doesn't that prove that general, domain-transcending creativity exists, independent of the field in which that creativity is applied?

No, and this question points to a common misunderstanding of what domain specificity claims. In fact, if one assumes that creativity is domain specific, one would expect – and domain specificity theory indeed predicts – the existence of polymaths. Just not a lot of them. Even if creativity were *completely* domain specific – even if intelligence, educational opportunities, material resources, and anything else that might help people be generally more creative didn't matter at all – domain specificity would *still* expect there to be occasional polymaths.

Imagine dealing out four hands of fifty-two well-shuffled playing cards, as one would in bridge. It would be exceedingly rare, but sometimes one might find most, or even all, of the aces, kings, and queens in a single hand. (Bridge-playing readers are now getting excited. This would be equally likely to occur in one's opponent's hand, of course. And let's remember that getting dealt all twelve of the two's, three's, and four's in a single hand is just as likely as getting all twelve aces, kings, and queens.) It would be somewhat less rare, but still extremely unusual, for most of just the aces and kings, or just the kings and queens, to be in a single hand (and getting all four aces is something most bridge players will experience at some point).

Such clustering of most of the high cards wouldn't happen very often, but it should happen on occasion. Being random (or more to the point, being uncorrelated) doesn't mean similar things don't sometimes get clumped together. In the same way, if being creative in fifty-two (or any number of) different areas were randomly distributed among a large population, one would expect occasions in which we would find people who are creative – even highly creative – in many different areas. It just wouldn't happen that often.

On the other hand, if "creativity" as a domain-general personal attribute existed – whether as a personality trait, a way of thinking, a cognitive skill, or some combination of things – then being creative in one domain would predict being creative in other, unrelated domains. If creativity were truly domain general – if there were some skills, general ways of thinking, personality traits, or anything else that tended to promote creativity across the board – then one would expect there to be a *lot* of polymaths, people who were creative geniuses (or at least near-geniuses) in many areas.

How many such people do you know, or even know of?

But What about Intelligence?

I've ignored the specter of intelligence as long as possible, but it must be acknowledged. The construct of general intelligence, whatever one believes about it, causes no problem for the idea I'm advancing. It even provides an illustrative contrast. I hate to raise it, however, because it can be such a contentious issue. Let's deal with it so that we can move on.

Intelligence – general intelligence, the kind of thing IQ tests are designed to measure – raises two questions in the context of creativity theory:

(1) *Is intelligence linked to creativity?* and
(2) *Might creativity be a general trait or skill in the same way that intelligence is believed by most psychologists to be a general, domain-transcending set of abilities?*

In answering these two questions, let's assume, for the sake of argument, that general intelligence – a set of cognitive abilities that influence how well one is able to do or to learn a wide variety of things across many domains, something psychologists call g – is real (because if it's not real, then there are no questions to answer). Let me answer these two question one at a time.

(1) *Is intelligence linked to creativity?* There are two answers to this question:
    (a) Probably yes, at least to some degree.
    (b) It doesn't matter, at least in regard to the issue of the domain generality or specificity of creativity.

Let's start with (a). Because creativity in many domains requires the kinds of skills and knowledge that g helps one acquire, there is certainly at least a small positive correlation between g and creativity in those domains. The impact of general intelligence on creativity in many domains might be small (and in others large), but assuming that g affects how well one learns a wide variety of things, there is likely to be at least a small positive impact on creativity in those domains.

So general intelligence, as measured by g, probably has some correlation with creativity in many domains. In some domains the correlation might be significant, in others tiny. This is an empirical question, but one we can't (yet) answer very well because past efforts to look for such linkages have generally assumed creativity is domain general and have therefore used what they thought were domain-general measures of creativity (like the Torrance or other DT tests) in their research.

Using domain-specific measures of creativity, however, it would be possible to assess just how significantly g is linked to creativity on a domain-by-domain basis. It is even possible that in some domains g will be found to be negatively linked to creativity, at least for some ranges of g (e.g., among those with above-average intelligence, or among those with IQ scores above a certain level [say 130], g might be negatively correlated with creative performance). But because most researchers have assumed that creativity is domain general, they have been asking a question – *Is intelligence linked to creativity?* – that has no real answer because there is no such thing as (general) creativity. As a result, research of this kind will report answers that will tend to vary depending on which measures of creativity one happens to select.

That leaves us to consider the second answer to the question, *Is intelligence linked to creativity?* That second answer – (b) It doesn't matter, at least in regard to the issue of the domain generality or specificity of creativity – focuses on what it would mean if answer (a) given above is true. Answer (b) claims that even if there is a link of some kind between IQ test scores (or general intelligence, however measured) and many kinds of creativity, it would tell us nothing about the domain specificity or domain generality of creativity.

But surely if IQ test scores and creative performance in most domains were positively correlated – or even going to the stronger cause-effect claim that g (general intelligence) has at least a modest impact on creativity across many domains – then creativity across domains would also show at least a modest positive correlation, would it not? No argument there; it would. And if g is positively correlated, even minimally, with creativity not just in many but in most domains, would that not be evidence that there is something that holds creativity together, something that shows general creativity does exist?

Not really. If g is the only common thread holding creativity together as a general trait, then the concept of creativity would add nothing to our understanding of that linkage beyond what g can already tells us. It would be like saying that the common thread that my list of creative geniuses share is that they are human. True, but that doesn't tell us anything, at least not anything very interesting. The concept of domain-general creativity requires that there be something more, some *additional* general trait or skill that predicts creativity above and beyond the ability of g (or the fact of being human) to predict creativity. So whether or not g is correlated positively with actual creative performance would tell us nothing about the domain generality (or domain specificity) of creativity.

The answer, then, to the first question that opened this section (*Is intelligence linked to creativity?*) is that whether the answer is yes or no – whether there is some linkage or not – simply doesn't matter, at least in the context of the argument I'm making. If intelligence (however measured) and creativity are not linked, then there is nothing more to be said. And if they are linked, that does indeed tell us something about intelligence and creativity: It tells us that, like grades in school, performance in many jobs, and measures of success in many domains, g also is associated with creativity in many domains. But if that is all there is to the domain generality of creativity, then there's nothing (at least nothing that is domain general) for the field of creativity research to study, test, or promote, no domain-general creative-thinking skills or traits of any kind, just general intelligence, which is already being studied intensively in another much older branch of psychology. This would add nothing interesting regarding the question of whether or not there is something other than g that predicts creativity across domains. (This is perhaps why some advocates of DT testing have taken great pains to point out that DT test scores generally have only very modest correlations with IQ test scores. It is only whatever is *not* simply an effect of g – and therefore only what DT tests could tell us that IQ tests have not already told us – that would be of interest in assessing students' creativity.)

The second question (*Might creativity be a general trait in the same way that intelligence is a general, domain-transcending set of abilities?*) is a more interesting one. Again, for the sake of argument, let's assume that g is what most psychologists think it is, a domain-general set of abilities that (together with many domain-specific abilities) influence how well one learns or can do many different kinds of things. (Again, if g doesn't actually exist, it won't matter. It's just the idea that there *might* be a domain-general set of abilities that affect performance across domains that we're interested in.) Could there be some general set of abilities or traits – let's call them c – that influence one's creativity across a wide range of otherwise unrelated domains (and above and beyond what g might be able to predict)?

This is the theory behind almost all creativity testing and most popular conceptions of creativity. But this is an empirical question, not a theoretical one. Whether creativity (as a skill or trait that leads to creative performance) is one thing or many very different things – whether it operates in a general way across domains or is collection of essentially unrelated skills or traits useful only in specific domains – is not an issue that can be decided by armchair reflection. The way to resolve it is through empirical studies.

The question can be framed in different ways, such as:

(1) Are people who are creative in one area also likely to be creative doing other, unrelated things?

(2) Can we predict a person's creativity in a domain based on their creativity in other domains?

(3) Are there at least modest positive correlations among different creative behaviors?

These three questions all ask essentially the same thing; questions 1 and 2 are really, like question 3, about correlations. So to test for domain specificity or domain generality, all one needs to do is get creativity ratings of things people have created in several different domains. To the extent those ratings are correlated, creativity must be domain general. If those ratings are not correlated, then creativity must be domain specific.

Evidence of Domain Specificity

Before I was a creativity researcher I was a creativity trainer. Programs like the ones I conducted were based on the assumption that the skills we were teaching would be applicable across domains. I wasn't training students to be creative poets, creative musicians, creative engineers, or creative scientists. I was training them to be creative in all those things and more – in *everything* they did. I believed the exercises and strategies and ways of approaching problems that I taught my students would help them be more creative, period.

So, as I mentioned briefly in the opening section, I set out to prove, with the help of a grant from the National Science Foundation, that creativity was domain general, at least to a considerable degree. I knew creativity wasn't *entirely* domain general; a person's education and experience in a particular domain would also matter. But I was certain that I would find a large domain-general component to creativity.

I was wrong. Rarely have I seen research results that were so clear and so consistent. In study after study, what I found was the exact opposite of what I had expected to find. Creativity in one domain simply didn't predict creativity in other domains, unless of course the two domains were very closely related.

Domain generality failed, and failed miserably. Creativity, both in my many studies and in those of others who ran their own independent investigations – some designed expressly to show why my earlier studies must have been wrong – kept coming to the same conclusion: low-to-nonexistent correlations across domains. Which translates directly to domain specificity. When it came to general, domain-transcending creativity, there was simply no there there.

These studies weren't based on creativity test scores, although such tests also point to domain specificity because they, too, tend not to be very highly correlated with one another. In fact, even Torrance, whose two eponymous creativity tests are the most widely used both in schools and until recently in research, found that his two tests of creativity had essentially zero correlation with each other. That is, no relationship at all.

Most people aren't aware of this. As commonly used and understood, the two Torrance Tests of Creative Thinking are both supposedly measuring the same thing, general creativity, just getting at it different ways. Which of the two tests researchers and gifted programs use, the figural or the verbal, is often more a matter of convenience than anything else (Baer, 2016; Kim, 2017). But as Cramond et al. (2005) noted in their "40-Year Follow-Up of the Torrance Tests of Creative Thinking":

> Responses to the verbal and figural tests of the TTCT are not only expressed in two different modalities – written or oral responses for the verbal, and drawn responses on the figural – but they are also measures of different creative abilities. In fact, Torrance (1990) found very little correlation ($r = .06$) between performance on the verbal and figural tests. (p. 284)

So although both tests are called tests of creative thinking and are often used interchangeably in both research and in selecting students for gifted education programs, the "creative thinking" that one of the Torrance Tests of Creative Thinking is measuring is not the same "creative thinking" that the other Torrance Test of Creative Thinking is measuring.

This would not have surprised Paul Torrance, who not only knew that scores on his two tests were uncorrelated, but who also argued that general scores (the Creativity Index) on the tests should not be used because they were likely to provide untrustworthy information:

> Torrance has discouraged the use of composite scores for the TTCT. He warned that using a single score like a composite score may be misleading because each subscale score has an independent meaning.
> (Kim et al., 2006, p. 461)

But it is precisely those Creativity Index scores that are most commonly used both in research and by gifted education programs. (In research, often not even the full test is given, just pieces of it, with the score on that one or those few parts of the test used as a stand-in for general creative-thinking ability.)

It's rather amazing that the lack of correlation (or the very low correlations) between different creativity tests has been commented on so rarely. If two intelligence tests had just a 0.06 correlation, would that be a matter of indifference? Surely it would indicate that something was amiss. If g is something real and two tests of it were essentially unrelated, one would assume that either one or both of the tests was not measuring *g*. At most, then, only one of the two Torrance Tests could be measuring general creativity. More likely, they are each measuring a limited skill that may (at most) influence creative performance in only a single, limited domain.

The lack of significant positive correlations among many creativity test scores supports arguments for domain specificity, but it isn't creativity test scores that really matter. What matters is actual creative performance, and that's what most of the research focused on the domain-generality/specificity question has looked at.

The basic format of these studies has been to ask participants to create a variety of artifacts. Having participants create things like poems, stories, and collages is most common because everyone can create such things to some degree rather easily (unlike, say, creating a symphony, an architectural design, or an original chemistry experiment, which most of us could not do at all), but many other tasks have also been employed in these studies. Experts from each domain are then asked to rate the creativity of those poems, stories, collages, etc., for creativity (e.g., for poetry, poets, poetry critics, and literature professors would qualify as experts; for collages, artists, art critics, and art teachers would be appropriate judges). The experts work independently and have no opportunity to discuss the things they've been asked to rate for creativity. In fact, the experts not only never meet as a group or have any opportunity to discuss the things they are judging. They usually don't even know who the other experts in the study might be.

This technique, called the Consensual Assessment Technique, was developed in 1982 by Teresa Amabile (see her 1996 book for details of the development and validation procedures). Over the ensuing decades the Consensual Assessment Technique has been further validated and extended by numerous researchers and is frequently called the "gold standard" of creativity assessment – mostly because it is the best, but perhaps also because it is very expensive in terms of the time and resources needed to employ it.

There have been three consistent results from studies in which participants have created multiple artifacts in different domains and those artifacts have been judged by appropriate experts in those domains, both in my studies and in those of other researchers:

- Experts tend to agree, in their respective domains, about what is more and what is less creative, even when they make those judgments without any opportunity to compare notes or confer with others. This is called inter-rater reliability, and there are statistical techniques for measuring it. The results – the coefficient alphas, as these measures of inter-rater agreement are called – are almost always quite high, typically between 0.70 and 0.90. (1.00 would mean perfect agreement.)

This is not surprising. Being an expert in a domain means that one shares knowledge, understandings, and values related to that domain with other experts in the field. Experts' judgments of what is more or less creative in their domain should be fairly consistent, particularly when dealing with artifacts that are not on the cutting edge of their fields, and research shows that they are indeed very consistent.

- High positive correlations are typical when participants complete more than one task in the same domain (e.g., studies in which participants write two or more poems, which are then judged for creativity independently). This is true even when the different tasks were undertaken at different times – as much as a year apart – and when different groups of experts have rated the creativity of the different artifacts.

  This is also not surprising. People who write creative poems today are more likely than chance to write creative poems tomorrow (or next year), and people who make creative collages today are more likely than chance to make creative collages tomorrow (or next year). There are certainly one-hit wonders in all fields, but they tend to be the exception, not the rule. The odds that a dramatist would write *Hamlet* and then go on to write nothing but totally pedestrian plays are slim.

- The correlations between creativity ratings *across* domains – this is the test for domain generality/specificity – hover around 0, *showing almost no domain generality at all*. This is especially true when participants also took IQ tests and differences attributable to IQ differences are statistically removed. Except for a very small domain-general effect of IQ, these studies have consistently given no evidence of domain generality of creativity. In study after study, creativity has shown itself to be highly domain specific. (Note: detailed citations for each of these points can be found in Baer, 2016, but are too numerous to list here. A few will be described in greater detail below and cited there.)

The basic format of those studies was this: Participants were asked to create two or more things in different domains. The participants in different studies varied in age, as did the things they were asked to create. Many of the studies involved writing stories and poems and creating collages, and none required levels of expertise that would not be common among all participants.

All of the tasks were thus possible, things that all participants were capable of doing, although at varying levels of skill. No specialized training, materials, or skill was required to complete any of the tasks. No group was asked, for example, to sculpt, develop a scientific theory, or write the score for an opera. The goal was to have the participants create things in different domains. Even first-grade students, for example, could make collages using pre-cut shapes, glue, and posterboard, and they could also create stories by telling what happens in a picture book with an ambiguous plot.

In one study with eighth-grade students, for example, fifty participants created poems, stories, mathematical word problems, and interesting equations (in which students were asked to create a mathematical equality that they considered especially interesting; see Baer, 1993, pp. 49–52, for more complete details on the tasks). Each student created one artifact in each category. There were two groups of twenty-five participants, with the order in which participants did the tasks reversed. Then the things the students had created were all judged for creativity by experts in the appropriate domains. The experts didn't know who had created the things they were judging or the purpose of the study. They did know the ages of the participants as a group (not individually). In a little more detail:

> Students' responses to these four creativity tests were typed and photo-copied by the experimenter and then rank ordered for creativity by five qualified experts, who were paid for their work. The expertise of the judges depended on the test. For example, the poems were rated by poets and English teachers, and the equations were judged by mathematics teachers and mathematics professors. (Baer, 1993, p. 50)

The inter-rater reliabilities (coefficient alpha) of these four sets of fifty papers were 0.78 (word problem), 0.86 (poems), 0.89 (stories), and 0.92 (equations). This showed that the judges, although working totally independently and with no possibility of conferring with other judges, agreed in their rankings.

There were six cross-domain correlations. Half of these were positive and half were negative, with a mean correlation of 0.06 and with just one of the six reaching statistical significance, as shown in Table 1. (Adjusted for multiple comparisons, even the one statistically significant result did not reach a 0.05 level of confidence.)

Table 1 Correlations among creativity ratings

Task	Poetry	Story	Word problem	Equation
Poetry	–	0.23	0.31*	−0.14
Story		–	0.20	−0.03
Word problem			–	−0.20

$N = 50$ * $p < 0.05$, two-tailed

I hypothesized that general intellectual ability might add to cross-domain correlations, and so I statistically removed variance attributable to math and verbal ability using standardized test scores. Once again there were three positive and three negative correlations, this time with a mean correlation of − 0.05. The only statistically significant correlation found after variance attributable to measures of general intellectual ability had been removed was a negative one, as shown in Table 2. (When adjusted for multiple comparisons, this also fell below the 0.05 level of confidence.)

Other researchers had similar results. For example, Han (2003) had 109 second-grade students complete a story-telling task (language), a collage-making task (art), and a math word-problem task (math). These tasks came from and had been validated using Amabile's (1996) guidelines for selecting appropriate tasks for a consensual assessment.

Han reported just one statistically significant ($p = 0.04$) correlation across domains (story-telling and math problem; $r = 0.283$, accounting for 8 percent of total variance). No measures of general intellectual ability were used in this study so the influence of general intelligence, which may have accounted for some of that variance, could not be assessed. No correction for multiple comparisons was conducted, which would likely have pushed the 0.04 value beyond the standard 0.05 cut-off for statistical significance – and in doing so change their results from *almost* no support for domain generality to no support at all. (A correction for multiple comparisons is a fairly new statistical technique that has become standard procedure in recent years when a statistical analysis involves multiple simultaneous statistical tests. It recognizes that such multiple comparisons make it likely that there will be some false positives – results that look statistically significant, but are actually just random error – when several tests are conducted using the same data set.)

Using an older population as participants, Ruscio et al. (1998) asked undergraduate students to complete three tasks – structure-building, collage-making, and poetry-writing. They also reported very little evidence of general creativity

Table 2 Partial correlations among creativity rating with variance attributable to math and verbal ability removed

Task	Poetry	Story	Word problem	Equation
Poetry	–	−0.01	0.19	−0.14
Story		–	0.05	0.07
Word problem			–	−0.45*

$N = 50$ * $p < 0.01$, two-tailed

(correlations of 0.18, 0.09, and –0.02 across domains). As with Han's study, one of the three correlations (the correlation between structure-building and collage-making) reached the 0.05 level of statistical significance ($r = 0.18$, accounting for a little more than 3 percent of the total variance). This was also not corrected for multiple comparisons.

But it is not clear that Ruscio et al.'s finding is evidence for domain generality even if it could survive a correction for multiple comparisons, because two of the tasks (structure-building and collage-making) may not actually be from two distinct domains but rather from the same general thematic area, and this was the only correlation that was statistically significant. The instructions for the two tasks were "build an aesthetically appealing structure that's at least fifteen inches tall" (p. 248) and "make a collage out of the materials you see in front of you" (p. 249). In each case subjects were directed to create a work of art given a set of materials. It is hard to interpret Ruscio et al.'s results as evidence of domain generality because the only commonality found among the creative performances of subjects on different tasks was between tasks that could be seen as coming from the same general thematic area. There were thus no positive correlations of measures of creative performance *across* domains.

In a similar fashion, Runco (1989) found low correlations (median $r = 0.18$) among the different kinds of works of art produced by his subjects. Even within the domain of art, different kinds of art performance yielded only a modest degree of generality across tasks. This is similar to the results reported by Ruscio et al. (1998) and offered no evidence of truly domain-general creativity.

In the hope of finding that perhaps creativity training worked more generally than these studies suggested, I designed a study in which I ran a week-long creativity-training workshop in a middle school that focused on a single domain and then looked to see if that training resulted in higher creativity not only in that domain, but also in other domains. The workshop consisted primarily of a series of poetry-relevant DT exercises. (The control group received training that was unrelated to creativity.) All participants later wrote both poems and stories for their regular classroom teachers. These poems and stories were then rated for creativity by panels of experts who knew nothing about the training sessions.

The participants who had taken part in the poetry-relevant DT training wrote markedly more creative poems than the control group, so the training worked in that regard. Their short stories were no more creative than those of untrained subjects, however. Once again, domain specificity won the day. Participants' creativity in the area of the training increased significantly ($p < 0.001$), but there was no statistically significant effect on their creativity in other domains (Baer, 1996).

This 1996 training study was something of a last-ditch attempt to find some thread of domain generality in the kinds of creativity training I and others had done for many years. I had designed and run many earlier correlational studies in the 1980s and early 1990s with the goal of demonstrating domain generality, but had failed miserably. I had found only domain specificity, which was not at all what I had either wanted or expected to find, but it was an outcome that stubbornly refused to be ignored.

These unanticipated results had been hard for me to swallow, and it was hard for other researchers to accept this outcome as well. One team of researchers, assuming I must have done something wrong or had somehow gotten a series of freak and unreliable results, conducted a rather large study with the goal of showing how wrong I had been (Conti et al., 1996; and yes, although they didn't suggest I had done anything wrong, in their paper's introduction on p. 385 they made it clear that their goal had been to overturn my earlier findings). They had participants do a total of seven tasks – three art activities and four writing activities. Each activity earned a creativity score for that specific task: four stories, rated independently for creativity, and three different kinds of artistic production, also rated for creativity independently. There were also two summed domain-based creativity scores, one for the four writing activities and one for the three art activities. This provided a total of twenty cross-domain comparisons, the ones that would show domain generality if there were any domain generality there to be found.

What did they find? Nothing; not a single one of the twenty cross-domain comparisons resulted in a statistically significant correlation. Chance alone would suggest that one of the twenty might have appeared to be correlated, even if that finding were actually no more than a random effect, but there were none. Zero. Zero for twenty.

In contrast, on the many *within*-domain comparisons the results came out just the way everyone – both theorists arguing for domain generality and those arguing for domain specificity – expected. The researchers looked to see if people who were creative on one art task were also likely to be creative on other arts tasks (they were), and whether creative performance on any one writing task predicted creative performance on each of the other writing tasks (it did). In fact, every one of these comparisons was statistically significant, so the materials they used seemed to work.

But those results – showing that creativity on one task in a domain predicted creativity on other tasks *in the same domain* – were predicted by both domain generality and domain specificity. Everyone expects people who write creative stories today to be more likely than chance to write creative stories tomorrow. Ditto for art tasks. Those results tell us nothing about domain specificity or generality.

In contrast, in the key comparisons – the twenty comparisons about which the two theories made *different* predictions – the score was clear: Domains specificity 20, Domain generality 0.

In *Varieties of (Scientific) Creativity: A Hierarchical Model of Domain-Specific Disposition, Development, and Achievement,* Simonton (2009, p. 441) noted that "A recurrent issue in the study of creativity is whether the phenomenon is domain specific or domain general (e.g., Simonton, 2007; Sternberg, 2005). Can psychologists plausibly speak of a generic creative process that transcends the particular problem-solving tasks of any given domain?" (p. 441). He studied domains and subdomains in the area of science and argued that they "can be ordered into a hierarchy ranging from the 'hard' natural sciences to the 'soft' social sciences" (p. 441). Whether or not such ordering is possible in other domains is an open question (Simonton argued that it should be possible), but either way, his hierarchy of scientific disciplines emphasizes the different natures of these fields and the possibility that the traits and abilities that lead to extreme creativity in one field may be very different from the traits and abilities found in eminent creators in other disciplines.

Feist (2004) commented that it is

> a very appealing, and ultimately firmly American, notion that a creative person could be creative in any domain he or she chose. All the person would have to do would be to decide where to apply her or his talents and efforts, practice or train a lot, and *voilà*, you have creative achievement. On this view, talent trumps domain and it really is somewhat arbitrary in which domain the creative achievement is expressed (p. 57).

Although the idea is appealing, especially to a creativity trainer like myself who wants to believe he is promoting his students' creativity in all that they do, Feist concluded that "this is a rather naïve and ultimately false position and that creative talent is in fact domain specific . . . creativity and talent are usually not among the domain general skills" (p. 57).

"The general consensus among creativity researchers is that creativity is largely domain specific," Sawyer (2015, p. 7) summarized in his widely used textbook. This means creativity training must also be domain specific:

> Research shows that creativity training is more effective when it focuses on a specific domain. Mayer (1989) found that when students were taught learning strategies that encouraged them to identify relational statements

and to extract generalizations from texts and problem statements, they displayed greater creativity. His research suggests that schools should "teach creative learning skills within specific content domains rather than as a separate course in general learning skills" (p. 204). Jay and Perkins (1997) found that training in problem finding, in a specific domain, worked. Dow and Mayer (2004) found that the most effective training was domain-specific. (Sawyer, 2015, p. 7)

Scott et al. (2004) reported the results of their meta-analysis of creativity-training research over the preceding half century. Their review included seventy published and peer-reviewed studies. They concluded that "more successful programs were likely to focus on development of cognitive skills and the heuristics involved in skill application, using realistic exercises *appropriate to the domain at hand*" (p. 361, italics added for emphasis). "The most clear-cut finding to emerge in the overall analysis was that the use of domain-based performance exercises was positively related ($r = .31$, $\beta = .35$) to effect size" (p. 380). The more domain specific the training, the more successful that training was.

In 1998 the *Creativity Research Journal* held its first (and to date only) Point/ Counterpoint debate (Baer, 1998; Plucker, 1998). The topic was the domain generality or specificity of creativity. The person who wrote for the domain-generality side of the debate started his defense by pretty much acknowledging that the tide of research had turned in favor of a domain-specific view:

> Recent observers of the theoretical (Csikszentmihalyi, 1988) and empirical (Gardner, 1993; Runco, 1989; Sternberg & Lubart, 1995) creativity literature could reasonably assume that the debate is settled in favor of content specificity. In fact, Baer (1994a, 1994b, 1994c) provided convincing evidence that creativity is not only content specific but is also task specific within content areas (Plucker, 1998, p. 179).

Indeed the tide had turned, and research since that 1998 debate has done nothing to turn it back. Although the field sometimes seems unready to acknowledge it – to do so would require that creativity researchers invalidate (or at least seriously review and question the findings of) decades of research that was based on the domain-generality assumption – the evidence seems too clear to deny, even to advocates of more domain-general approaches.

I had to give up on domain generality and the fantasy that my training was promoting creativity across the board. Nothing is 100 percent, of course. As noted above, general intelligence may make a small domain-general contribution to creativity. But if one is interested in more than fringe effects, the story of creativity will need to be told in the context of domain specificity.

Conclusions: Creativity Research, Theory, Testing, and Training

Creativity Research and Theory

In 2013, Dobzhansky wrote an essay titled "Nothing in Biology Makes Sense Except in the Light of Evolution." Grand theories like Darwin's are powerful and awe-inspiring. They bring so much of what we know together, connecting things that seem so far-flung as to be in different worlds – literally:

> The goal of NASA's Exobiology program (formerly Exobiology and Evolutionary Biology) is to understand the origin, evolution, distribution, and future of life in the Universe. Research is centered on the origin and early evolution of life, the potential of life to adapt to different environments, and the implications for life elsewhere.[3]

Evolution isn't just a flimsy umbrella that provides no more than a superficial connection between such diverse things as "the origin, evolution, distribution, and future of life in the Universe" or that connects all living things here on Earth in only the most cursory and insignificant way. The theory of evolution through natural selection is deeply meaningful, the very opposite of the gossamer-thin standard definition of creativity (the one that says that something must be novel or original and also useful or appropriate to the goal of the creator in order to be deemed creative). This definition of creativity offers almost no insight into its subject. Neither do any of the theories based on it.

The theory of evolution through natural selection helps us understand things that are otherwise unfathomable; it helps us make predictions and guides us toward what it is we should be looking for in truly diverse arenas. Not so any current theory of creativity.

It would certainly be wonderful to have a majestic theory of creativity, one that would allow us to learn and say powerful things about creativity of all kinds, what its essence is and what skills or other attributes lead to it regardless of the domain or the level (big-C genius-level creativity or little-c everyday creativity).

But no such theory is possible in creativity. It isn't that we just haven't yet discovered such a theory. A theory of that kind simply does not, and could not, exist, because there is no such thing as "creativity" (in the general sense) for such a theory to explain.

---

[3] https://astrobiology.nasa.gov/research/astrobiology-at-nasa/exobiology/

That can be a tough pill to swallow. The fact that our theories will be limited to specific domains (as well as other constraints) is humbling in exactly the opposite way that a grand theory like evolution is humbling. The latter fills us with wonder, while the former reminds us how limited our goals must be.

It would make the tasks of creativity theorists, creativity researchers, creativity trainers, and creativity testers easier if creativity were something that was in a meaningful way definable and localizable, if creativity were the same (or at least very similar in its essence) across domains and contexts. And it would be convenient if the skills, knowledge, attitudes, personality traits, and approaches that led to creativity in one kind of endeavor were at least roughly similar to the skills, knowledge, attitudes, personality traits, and approaches that lead to creativity in most other endeavors.

But, as we have seen, creativity is neither easy nor convenient in either sense. To understand or predict creative performance will require more fine-grained analyses and more limited theories.

Consider one issue that has bedeviled creativity theory and research: the connection between creativity and mental illness. Claims that the incidence of mental illness is higher among creative people is a mainstay in psychology that goes back to ancient Greece (Abraham, 2015; Becker, 2001; Ellis, 1926). "Few issues polarize the scientific community within the field of creativity as the purported association between creativity and psychopathology" (Abraham, 2014, p. 1). Conflicting research claims and very hard-to-resolve disputes regarding what constitutes appropriate data and how that data should be interpreted are common in this arena.

At least part of the difficulty in untangling many conflicting research claims about creativity is rooted in the domain-general nature of the research questions that have been posed. There does appear to be a significant positive correlation between genius-level creativity and mental illness in some fields, such as the arts. In other domains, however, such as the sciences, there appears to be no mental illness-creativity connection. As Simonton (2010) explained,

> the rate and intensity of adulthood symptoms vary according to the particular domains in which creative genius is expressed ... geniuses in the natural sciences tend to be more mentally healthy than in the social sciences; geniuses in the social sciences, more so than those in the humanities; and geniuses in the humanities, more so than those in the arts (pp. 226–228)

The differences extend down to subdomains, where distinct microdomain differences can be found. Within the field of creative writing, for example, highly acclaimed poets have been more likely to be diagnosed mentally ill than similarly famous fiction writers.

Several historiometric studies have found evidence of mental illness (often speculated to be mood disorder or depression) in poets compared with other writers ... and writers compared with both other artistic professions and nonartistic professions. (Taylor et al., 2017, p. 178)

Because researchers have typically sought large-scale, domain-general answers to the creativity-mental illness connection, contradictory results have been more the rule than the exception. When researchers have focused their target toward more domain-specific ways of thinking about possible mental illness-creativity connections, however, a much clearer understanding has emerged. As Taylor (2017) summarized based on her extensive meta-analysis:

One fundamental issue that the study highlights is the need for conclusions based on individual studies to be highly specific in regard to the approach being utilized and the type of disorder and domain of creativity being assessed. Asking if creativity is related to mood disorder is too general to yield constructive answers and may lead to faulty or overgeneralized conclusions. (p. 1067)

A few more examples will be instructive. Amabile's (1996) work in the area of intrinsic motivation has shown how important such motivation can be in creative performance and how extrinsic constraints can undermine such performance. But this work has been challenged by numerous studies that have produced contradictory results, as noted above (see, e.g., Cameron & Pierce, 1994 and Eisenberger & Shanock, 2003). The grand theory of intrinsic and extrinsic motivation's effects on creativity – that intrinsic motivation increases creativity and extrinsic motivation decreases it – is clearly too broad, but it does point us to an area that needs to be explored with a more fine-grained and targeted approach. Future research needs to help us understand the contexts in which each kind of motivation is most conducive to creative productivity.

Ditto for tools like brainstorming, which seem to be of value according to some studies but not others (Mullen et al., 1991). Are there contexts or domains in which brainstorming is reliably productive (or unproductive)? Rather than trying to answer global questions about the usefulness of brainstorming, a more modest agenda of answering such "It depends" questions could help us understand when and how best to use this tool, and when not to.

What about personality traits associated with creativity? For example, are creative people more or less conscientious than less creative people? The answer here is quite clear: It depends. Creativity research has suggested that conscientiousness has a significant positive impact on creativity in some domains (such as some scientific fields) and a significant negative impact in others (such as some artistic fields; Feist, 1998, 1999). So conscientiousness both promotes and impedes creativity, depending on the domain.

Inconsistencies in personality research more generally may be the result of failing to attend to domain. As Taylor et al. (2017) noted:

> Based on a comprehensive review, Batey and Furnham (2006) suggest that inconsistent results in investigations of creativity and Eysenck's supertraits may be due to domain differences .... In sum, FFM [five-factor model] personality traits are differentially related to performance across different domains. (pp. 169–172)

Similarly, the values and value hierarchies of creative people have been shown to vary widely across domains, a fact that has been hidden in past research that used a general or global creativity score and connected that score to participants' values. This is an approach that is "inconsistent with both creativity's movement toward a domain-specific viewpoint, and [recent research suggesting that] the relationship between values and the frequency of creative behaviors differs by domain" (Taylor & Kaufman, 2021, p. 501).

Surely the values held by more creative people should matter to us. But as in so many other areas, most research on the values of more and less creative people has largely ignored domains, assuming that creativity was one unified thing with a single set of tools, approaches, traits, motivations, and values associated with it. We now know that creativity is many distinct and essentially unrelated things, each supported by its own distinct array of tools, approaches, traits, motivations, and values that vary widely by domain. As a result, research on the values that undergird creativity based on a domain-general conception of creativity has resulted in a false picture of what it means to be creative:

> The value hierarchies for the different domains assessed were not consistent with either past studies or with each other in predictable ways. This finding suggests that collapsing the creative scores of different types of tasks into one general creativity quotient may be erroneous and yield results that primarily reflect artistic creativity. Thus, we would argue this practice should be avoided in future values studies .... [I]t makes sense that people who are drawn to be creative in different domains would show different types of values. (Taylor & Kaufman, 2021, pp. 512–513)

"Collapsing" domains of creativity when considering value hierarchies associated with creativity in diverse domains can, from a researcher's perspective, be a very convenient approach, but it leads to the same kinds of errors and misunderstandings that Plato's (and many others') "craving for generality" has caused. And once such research has been published and confirmed through replication – replication based on the same false domain-general model – it is hard to undo the damage.

Consider DT. Tests of DT have sometimes been shown to relate to creative performance and sometimes not. As explained above, Plucker's (1999) extensive reanalysis of the validity data offered for the Torrance Tests found that verbal TTCT scores *did* predict creative performance but figural TTCT scores did *not* predict the same outcomes. That the two tests made different predictions should not be a surprise, of course, because Torrance's own data showed that the two tests were essentially uncorrelated and that whatever things the two tests are measuring, they are two very different things.

Plucker explained these results as an effect a "linguistic bias in the adult creative achievement checklists" (1999, p. 110), an effect, that is to say, of domain specificity. The verbal DT test predicted verbal creativity, but the figural DT test did not predict verbal creativity. This does not mean that the tests are worthless, or even that the verbal test is "better" than the figural test. What it suggests is that DT tests may have validity as predictors of creative performance *in limited domains.* They are not tests of creativity, but might be predictors of creativity in particular domains.

This in turns opens the door to the possibility that DT, as long ago proposed, is indeed at least sometimes a component of creative thinking, but that DT is very domain specific, and perhaps context specific as well. DT may matter – it may lead to actual creative performance – only in some domains or only in some contexts. In which domains or contexts creativity is supported by domain-specific DT is something that only detailed research can confirm or deny, however. The answer is not simply yes or no.

What does seem clear is that DT, like creativity, is domain specific (as Torrance showed), whether or not it promotes creativity in its respective domain. DT ability related to domain-specific content may well be extremely important (that is, related to creative performance) in some domains and modestly (or just slightly) important in others. It might not be at all helpful in still others, and there is at least the theoretical possibility that it could be negatively correlated with creativity in some few domains. And the relationship between some kinds of DT ability and some kinds of creative achievement may be quite complex, with increases in DT ability past a point becoming counterproductive. Runco et al. (2010), for example, reported that:

> The relationship between TTCT indexes and personal achievement seemed to indicate an optimal level of divergent thinking, at least in the regression showing the quadratic trend. This, too, makes a great deal of sense in that thinking divergently probably could be taken too far and as such led to wild, crazy, and useless ideas. (p. 366)

These are interesting empirical questions awaiting thoughtful research.

Because creativity does not exist as a set of domain-general skills, the answer to many questions in the area of creativity will likely be, both now and forever, "It depends." The answer may depend on many things, the domain being especially significant. Conducting creativity research as if creativity were one thing (or one group of things) that transcends domains is to invite confusion, contradiction, and a general failure to make progress. This is true, as we have seen, with much of the creativity research conducted during the past half century. It is equally likely to be true regarding what has the potential – if it could find ways to avoid the pitfall of assuming that creativity is one thing rather than many things – to become ground-breaking new research using brain imaging and other neurocognitive research tools. But this has, thus far, not been what has been done. "Despite these glaring problems, we continue to carry out neurocognitive investigations on creativity across domains and make generalizations about how this is indicative of creative thinking in general" (Abraham, 2012, p. 21).

Domain-general theories of creativity and the research those theories inspire will, as we have seen, generally disappoint. Conducting creativity research domain by domain is more labor-intensive that it would be if very general theories were possible, and it is certainly hard work. If we want to avoid conflicting research results that prove X in one study but not-X in the next, however, attending to domains, attending to contexts, and attending to special circumstances will be necessary.

That is not to say that there is no place at all for more general theories. Metatheories that transcend domains and provide heuristics that help guide us to productive domain-specific theories and approaches to creativity are still possible. The discussion above of DT as a domain-specific skill is instructive here. Although DT tests have been shown not to have domain-general predictive validity, the concept of domain-specific DT can be used to guide investigations in diverse domains to learn where DT (and perhaps exercises designed to produce it, like brainstorming) might be productive.

Similarly, expertise will be a component of creativity in most domains, even though the nature of that expertise will vary quite widely. Kaufman and his colleagues have shown that in judging creativity in diverse domains, there are domains, such as poetry, that require considerably more expertise on the part of judges than others, such as short stories. The key test in these studies has been to compare the creativity judgments of novices with those of experts in a domain (Kaufman & Baer, 2012). Those studies have shown that there is great variability in the amount of expertise needed to make reliable and valid creativity judgments in different domains.

Kaufman and Beghetto's (2009) Four-C model and Simonton's (1999) Blind Variation and Selective Retention (BVSR) model might also be useful and in parallel ways help guide us to the more detailed, domain- and context-specific research that we should be conducting. Might, for example, BVSR describe creative productivity well in some domains and contexts but not in others?

Creativity Testing and Training, plus a Word about Folk Psychology

The issue of domain-specific testing has already been discussed above in the context of DT testing. DT is but one kind of creativity testing, however. Other kinds of creativity testing need also to attend to domains (and perhaps other constraints) and validated for specific uses. Because a test predicts creativity in one domain does not validate it for use in other domains. Plucker's (1999) work, as discussed in the previous section, is a prime example of this.

The Consensual Assessment Technique (Amabile, 1996), described above as the "gold standard" of creativity assessment, was not designed with domain specificity in mind. But the Consensual Assessment Technique does, in fact, assess creativity on specific tasks, which makes it ideal for some domain- and context-specific creativity research. Unfortunately, the Consensual Assessment Technique does not lend itself readily to standardization, which often makes it difficult to compare results across studies. It is also very resource intensive. Participants must actually create something, not just make lists. And then numerous experts must be cajoled into rating the creativity of each of those artifacts (and be compensated for their efforts).

It is interesting to note that Amabile's initial use of the Consensual Assessment Technique in discovering the impact of intrinsic and extrinsic constraints on creative performance implicitly assumed that whatever effect those constraints might have on creativity in one domain would also hold for creativity in any domain. As we have seen, however, the effects of intrinsic and extrinsic motivation are more complicated than that. It may be the case – and this is an area in which relatively little research has been conducted – that intrinsic motivation matters more in some domains than others, matters more at some levels (e.g., big-C versus little-c creativity) than others, or matters more with some groups of people than others.

There is a significant body of research, for example, suggesting that intrinsic and extrinsic motivation may have different impacts on creative performance on creative writing and collage-making tasks among middle school girls and boys, with girls suffering much greater decrements when extrinsic constraints are applied. Boys sometimes even see a boost in creativity under extrinsic constraints (Baer, 2016; Cameron & Pierce, 1994; Eisenberger & Shanock, 2003).

A similar gender difference has been observed in connections between creativity and mental illness among renowned poets. Although both groups show higher than average incidence of mental illness, female poets have significantly higher rates of mental illness than male poets. (It is important to note that this is true at the big-C, genius level of poetic creativity only; no such linkage has been reported for people writing poetry more generally.) It has been hypothesized that this difference might also be related to differences in responses to extrinsic constraints (Baer, 2016; Kaufman & Baer, 2002).

The power and usefulness of the Consensual Assessment Technique is especially apparent when considering what creativity ratings on a task in one domain might mean for creativity in other domains. The research on domain specificity/generality described above has shown quite clearly that these ratings are very domain specific and are neither measures of domain-general creativity nor measures of creativity in any domain other than the domain of the task used in the ratings. In the latter case it is of course possible that future research might show in rare cases that Consensual Assessment Technique creativity ratings in one domain also predict creative performance in some other domain, but that is an empirical question, not one that can be answered by an a priori assumption.

It is crucial that both researchers and those doing creativity testing for other purposes use domain- and situation-appropriate tests. Many gifted and talented programs, for example, use creativity assessment of some kind as part of their selection criteria. Either a Consensual Assessment Technique creativity rating of short stories or the verbal form of the Torrance Tests of Creative Thinking might be appropriate for admission decisions if the program is a creative writing program, but not if the focus of the program is mathematics or science (or tennis or basketball).

And then there is the issue of creativity training, which is what got me into the field of creativity research in the first place. As explained earlier, domain-general creativity training – what I once believed I was doing – is not possible.

> The consensus among creativity researchers is that although there are domain-general creative strategies, creativity is primarily domain specific. The implication of domain specific creativity research is that we can't hope to produce more creative graduates simply by adding creativity enrichment activities to the curriculum. If math and science continue to be taught in a way that doesn't foster creative thinking and problem solving, then no amount of creativity training or arts education can help. Rather, it will be necessary to transform the ways that each subject area is taught, so that the knowledge that students acquire is of the sort that fosters creative thinking and behavior. (Sawyer, 2015, p. 8)

The fact that creativity-relevant skills and knowledge vary from domain to domain does not mean that creativity training must focus on a single domain, however. That, of course, is one direction such training might take, for example in the case of a creative writing gifted and talented program. But what might seem like a more general approach to creativity training is still possible, as long as one uses multiple and diverse domains as the foci of the training. One might use activities that would promote creativity in domains X, Y, and Z – "providing a variety of domain-specific creativity training, in multiple contexts and task materials" (Sawyer, 2015, p. 7) – knowing that in doing so one would not have the same impact in any of those domains as one might if the training were limited to more intensive work concentrated in a single domain. Such training could nonetheless lead to modest improvements in creative performance in multiple domains, not because the training provided a domain-general improvement in creativity but simply because the training provided multiple domain-specific increases in creativity.

The issues above relate primarily to the work of creativity theorists, researchers, testers, and trainers. There is also a folk psychology of creativity that makes many of the same assumptions about creativity. I have had many students, both children and adults, tell me that they are not very creative. When I ask them what they mean, they explain that they don't write poetry and are not very good at art.

If I ask them about other things they do, I often find they are quite creative in other areas. These might be academic pursuits (e.g., creativity in solving math puzzles, originality in designing science experiments, or analytic insight in historical analysis) or nonacademic activities (e.g., creativity in teaching, in resolving disputes with friends, or in playing sports or other games). Creativity isn't something one either has or lacks without regard to the kinds of things one happens to be doing, but is instead something a person might demonstrate:

- in multiple and diverse ways;
- at a wide range of levels; and
- in all kinds of activities and settings.

Understanding this can be enlightening and liberating. It can sometimes change how people see themselves in significant ways.

(Why creativity has come to be associated more with the arts than nonartistic domains is a mystery. Even the APA participates in supporting this perception. The division of the Association that looks at creativity is Division 10: The Society for the Psychology of Aesthetics, Creativity and the Arts. While not ruling out creativity in areas other than aesthetics and the arts, the name does imply a special connection, does it not?)

Summing Up

We have seen that the "craving for generality" has distorted our understanding of creativity. It is not hard to understand this craving, of course. Grand theories like Darwin's evolution through natural selection and Einstein's general relativity are as rare as they are amazing. But creativity is not alone in being limited to theories of modest size.

Consider the brain. The brain is a very tangible, observable thing, and although there can be arguments about its bounds (e.g., is the eye part of the brain?) and we know that it is affected by all manner of internal and external events (e.g., "evidence for links between the composition of gut microbiomes and brain processes"; Thayer, 2021), its physical delineation is reasonably clear. Nonetheless, neuroscientists warn us that a general understanding of the brain may be an unreasonable goal.

> The nature of the brain – simultaneously integrated and composite – may mean that our future understanding will inevitably be fragmented and composed of different explanations for different parts. (Cobb, 2020, p. 371)

> Global understanding [of the brain], when it comes, will likely take the form of diverse panels loosely stitched together into a patchwork quilt. (Churchland & Abbott, 2016, p. 349)

So it will be with creativity – different explanations for different parts resulting in something like a loosely stitched patchwork quilt with no overall logic linking each tiny part with the rest. As Dietrich and Kanso (2010) argued:

> [C]reative thinking does not appear to critically depend on any single mental process or brain region . . . . To make creativity tractable in the brain, it must be further subdivided into different types that can be meaningfully associated with specific neurocognitive processes. (p. 822)

"Creativity" is an abstract concept, with no obvious lines of demarcation. It is not something nature has clearly carved at its joints, as Plato's *Phaedrus* argues must be the form of successful theories. But it should be no surprise that such an abstract concept is not a single thing that can be captured in a general theory or understanding, especially when one of the things creativity most depends on – the brain – is itself something that may require a fragmented understanding, a patchwork of loosely linked parts. That creativity is mysterious and multifaceted and impossible to bring together under a single framework should be no surprise.

But it nonetheless *is* to most people a surprise, one that flies in the face of what seems to many like common sense. It remains hard for the field of creativity research and theory to relinquish its long-held domain-generality assumption regarding creativity-relevant skills and personality attributes, just is it is hard to let go of one's "craving for generality" in one's conception of creativity as having some internal coherence and shared essence.

It is so much easier to stick with what may seem like common sense, even as we learn just how wrong that common sense (mis)understanding is, because of both (a) our long history of thinking of creativity as a unified concept and (b) the fact that it would make creativity researchers', theorists', trainers', and testers' work grander, more extensive, and as a consequence probably more satisfying if creativity were one thing rather than many. As Engber (2016) observed in looking at another troubled theory in psychology (ego depletion), "The diminution of the Big Idea isn't easy to accept, even for those willing to concede that there are major problems in their field."

What would the field of creativity research look like if the field let go of the myth of domain-general creativity? Here is the complete list of articles, minus one obituary and one commentary, from the 2020 *Journal of Expertise* (all issues of vol. 3):

Poker as a Domain of Expertise

Fluid Intelligence is Key to Successful Cryptic Crossword Solving

On the Empirical Substantiation of the Definition of "Deliberate Practice" (Ericsson et al., 1993) and "Deliberate Play" (Côté et al., 2007) in Youth Athletes

Esport Expertise Benefits Perceptual-Cognitive Skill in (Traditional) Sport

Influence of Expertise on the Visual Control Strategies of Athletes During Competitive Long Jumping

The Gaze Relational Index as a Measure of Visual Expertise

The Vanderbilt Holistic Processing Tests for Novel Objects: Validation in Novice Participants

Inter Sport Transfer: Experiences of High Performing Australian Adolescent Athletes

Influence of Experts' Domain-specific Knowledge on Risk Taking in Adversarial Situations

A Model of Information Use During Anticipation in Striking Sports (MIDASS)

Considerations for Application of Skill Acquisition in Sport: An Example from Tennis

Perceptual-motor Abilities Underlying Expertise in Esports

It Ain't What You Do – It's the Way That You Do It: Is Optimizing Challenge Key in the Development of Super-Elite Batsmen?

The domains under considerations included Cryptic Crossword Solving, Competitive Long Jumping, Tennis, Cricket, Esports, Visual Expertise, Poker, and Influence of Experts' Domain-specific Knowledge on Risk Taking in Adversarial Situations. The most general topic was Inter Sport Transfer (and even in that article, the possibility of domain generality was limited to transferring skills only among different sports, which is itself a fairly limited domain).

Compare these to the topics in any of the major creativity journals, which tend to focus on much more general skills. For example, here is the table of contents of the final 2020 issue of the *Creativity Research Journal* (vol. 32, issue 4):

Can Concept Mapping Facilitate Verbal Divergent Thinking?
A Distracted Muse: The Positive Effect of Dual-Task Distraction on Creative Potential
When Did Songwriters Write Their Best Songs?
School Students' Implicit Theories of Creativity and their Self Perceptions as Artists
The Impact of Educational Motivation and Self-acceptance on Creativity among High School Students
Factor Structure of Play Creativity: A New Instrument to Assess Movement Creativity
Employees' Attitudes and Values toward Creativity, Work Environment, and Job Satisfaction in Human Service Employees
Perceived Organizational Support and Employee Creativity: The Mediation Role of Calling
Implicit and Explicit Problem-Solving Process during Chinese Radical Assembly Game
The Effects of Religious Orientations on Malevolent Creativity: Role of Positive Emotions and Spiritual Intelligence
The Order–Chaos Dynamic of Creativity

Most of the articles were about creativity in general, not about creativity in a specific domain – although there were a few, which shows how possible such research can be.

Creativity research and theory need to follow the example of the psychology of expertise.

It would make the work of creativity researchers and trainers easier if creativity *were* some process or set of processes that led to more creativity in whatever one did. It would also be easier to understand creativity if there were some unifying attribute that creative products of all kinds shared. But just as there is no underlying attribute that describes all kinds of goodness (or all kinds of expertise) and no set of skills whose use typically results in good outcomes (or that constitute expertise) whatever the domain or context, creativity is far too complex, and far too mysterious, to be defined by or produced by following a simple formula.

If understanding, promoting, and assessing creativity really matter to us, we have to accept that no general theory of creativity is possible, that creativity has no overall logic, and that the most one can hope to find are adequate explanations of each of the things we lump together and label "creative." Things and ideas can be creative, in varying degrees, but not because creativity has been somehow injected into them. There is simply no such thing as creativity apart from those creative things and ideas.

Creativity is not some actual, independent, domain-transcending entity, something one can isolate for study, for measurement, or for general understanding. In the ways many of us would most like to think of creativity, it simply does not exist.

Creativity is much more interesting than that.

References

Abraham, A. (2012). The neuroscience of creativity: A promising or perilous enterprise? In A. P. Alejandre (ed.), *Creativity and Cognitive Neuroscience* (pp. 15–24). Madrid: Fundación Tomás Pascual y Pilar Gómez-Cuétera.

Abraham, A. (2014). Is there an inverted-U relationship between creativity and psychopathology? *Frontiers in Psychology, 5*, 750: 1–2.

Abraham, A. (2015). Madness and creativity – yes, no or maybe? *Frontiers in Psychology, 6*, 1055: 1–3.

Amabile, T. M. (1996). *Creativity in Context: Update to the Social Psychology of Creativity.* Boulder, CO: Westview.

Appiah, K. A. (2008). *Experiments in Ethics.* Cambridge, MA: Harvard University Press.

Baer, J. (1993). *Creativity and Divergent Thinking: A Task-specific Approach.* Hillsdale, NJ: Lawrence Erlbaum Associates.

Baer, J. (1996). The effects of task-specific divergent-thinking training. *Journal of Creative Behavior, 30*: 183–187.

Baer, J. (1998). The case for domain specificity in creativity. *Creativity Research Journal, 11*: 173–177.

Baer, J. (2016). *Domain Specificity of Creativity.* San Diego, CA: Academic Press/Elsevier.

Barbot, B. & Said-Metwaly, S. (2021). Is there really a creativity crisis? A critical review and meta-analytic re-appraisal. *The Journal of Creative Behavior, 55*(3): 696–709.

Bayle, P. (1705). *Pensées Diverses* (vol. 4). Rotterdam: Chez Reinier Leers.

Becker, G. (2001). The association of creativity and psychopathology: Its cultural-historical origins. *Creativity Research Journal, 13*(1): 45–53.

Boring E. G. (1923). Intelligence as the tests test it. *New Republic, 36*: 35–37.

Cameron, J. & Pierce, W. D. (1994). Reinforcement, reward, and intrinsic motivation: A meta-analysis. *Review of Educational Research, 64*: 363–423.

Churchland, A. K. & Abbott, L. F. (2016). Conceptual and technical advances define a key moment for theoretical neuroscience. *Nature Neuroscience, 19*(3): 348–349.

Cobb, M. (2020). *The Idea of the Brain: The Past and Future of Neuroscience.* New York: Basic Books.

Conti, R., Coon, H., & Amabile, T. M. (1996). Evidence to support the componential model of creativity: Secondary analyses of three studies. *Creativity Research Journal, 9*: 385–389.

Cramond, B., Matthews-Morgan, J., Bandalos, D., & Zuo, L. (2005). A report on the 40-year follow-up of the Torrance Tests of Creative Thinking. *Gifted Child Quarterly*, 49: 283–291.

Crockenberg, S. B. (1972). Creativity tests: A boon or boondoggle for education? *Review of Educational Research, 42*: 27–45.

Dietrich, A. & Kanso, R. (2010). A review of EEG, ERP, and neuroimaging studies of creativity and insight. *Psychological Bulletin, 136*(5): 822–848.

Dobzhansky, T. (2013). Nothing in biology makes sense except in the light of evolution. *The American Biology Teacher, 75*(2): 87–91.

Eisenberger, R. & Shanock, L. (2003). Rewards, intrinsic motivation, and creativity: A case study of conceptual and methodological isolation. *Creativity Research Journal, 15*: 121–130.

Ellis, H. (1926). *A Study of British Genius*. Boston, MA: Houghton Mifflin.

Engber, D. (2016). Everything is crumbling. *Slate*, 6. www.slate.com/articles/health_and_science/cover_story/2016/03/ego_depletion_an_influential_theory_in_psychology_may_have_just_been_debunked.html

Feist, G. J. (1998). A meta-analysis of personality in scientific and artistic creativity. *Personality and Social Psychology Review, 1998*: 290–309.

Feist, G. J. (1999). The influence of personality on artistic and scientific creativity. In R. J. Sternberg (ed.), *Handbook of Creativity* (pp. 273–296). New York: Cambridge University Press.

Feist, G. J. (2004). The evolved fluid specificity of human creative talent. In R. J. Sternberg, E. L. Grigorenko, & J. L. Singer (eds.), *Creativity: From Potential to Realization* (pp. 57–82). Washington, DC: American Psychological Association.

Glennan, S. (2017). *The New Mechanical Philosophy*. Oxford: Oxford University Press.

Gramsci, A. (2011). *Prison Notebooks Volume 2* (vol. 2). New York: Columbia University Press.

Guilford, J. P. (1950). Creativity. *American Psychologist, 5*: 444–454.

Han, K. S. (2003). Domain specificity of creativity in young children: How quantitative and qualitative data support it. *Journal of Creative Behavior, 37*: 117–142.

Kaufman, J. C. & Baer, J. (2002). I bask in dreams of suicide: Mental illness, poetry, and women. *Review of General Psychology, 6*: 271–286.

Kaufman, J. C. & Baer, J. (2012). Beyond new and appropriate: Who decides what is creative? *Journal of Creative Behavior, 24*: 83–91.

Kaufman, J. C. & Beghetto, R. A. (2009). Beyond big and little: The four c model of creativity. *Review of General Psychology, 13*(1): 1–12.

Kenny, A. (2008). *Wittgenstein*. Hoboken, NJ: John Wiley & Sons.

Kim, K. H. (2011). The creativity crisis: The decrease in creative thinking scores on the Torrance Tests of Creative Thinking. *Creativity Research Journal, 23*: 285–295.

Kim. K. H., Cramond, B., & Bandalos, D. L. (2006). The latent structure and measurement invariance of scores on the Torrance Tests of Creative Thinking-Figural. *Educational and Psychological Measurement, 66*: 459–477.

Kim, K. H. (2017). The Torrance tests of creative thinking – figural or verbal: Which one should we use? *Creativity. Theories–Research–Applications, 4* (2): 302–321.

Kuhn, T. S. (1970). *The Structure of Scientific Revolutions*. Chicago, IL: University of Chicago Press.

Moore, G. E. & Baldwin, T. (1993). *Principia Ethica*. New York: Cambridge University Press.

Mullen, B., Johnson, C., & Salas, E. (1991). Productivity loss in brainstorming groups: A meta-analytic integration. *Basic and Applied Social Psychology, 12*: 3–23.

Plucker, J. A. (1998). Beware of simple conclusions: The case for the content generality of creativity. *Creativity Research Journal, 11*: 179–182.

Plucker, J. A. (1999). Is the proof in the pudding? Reanalyses of Torrance's (1958 to present) longitudinal data. *Creativity Research Journal, 12*(2): 103–114.

Richards, R. L. (1976). A comparison of selected Guilford and Wallach-Kogan creative thinking tests in conjunction with measures of intelligence. *Journal of Creative Behavior, 10*(3): 151–164.

Robertson, R. (2011). *The Enlightenment: The Pursuit of Happiness, 1680–1790*. London: HarperCollins.

Rose, L. H. & Lin, H. (1984). A meta-analysis of long-term creativity training programs. *Journal of Creative Behavior, 18*: 11–22.

Runco, M. A. (1989). The creativity of children's art. *Child Study Journal, 19*: 177–190.

Runco, M. A. & Acar, S. (2012). Divergent thinking as an indicator of creative potential. *Creativity Research Journal, 24*(1): 66–75.

Runco, M. A., Millar, G., Acar, S., & Cramond, B. (2010). Torrance tests of creative thinking as predictors of personal and public achievement: A fifty-year follow-up. *Creativity Research Journal, 22*(4): 361–368.

Ruscio, J., Whitney, D. M., & Amabile, T. M. (1998). Looking inside the fishbowl of creativity: Verbal and behavioral predictors of creative performance. *Creativity Research Journal, 11*: 243–263.

Sawyer, K. (2012). *Explaining Creativity: The Science of Human Innovation (2nd* ed.). Oxford: Oxford University Press, p. 51.

Sawyer, R. K. (2015). How to transform schools to foster creativity. *Teachers College Record, 118* (4): 1–23. http://keithsawyer.com/publications/

Scott, G., Leritz, L. E., & Mumford, M. D. (2004). The effectiveness of creativity training: A quantitative review. *Creativity Research Journal, 16* (4): 361–388.

Simonton, D. K. (1999). Creativity as blind variation and selective retention: Is the creative process Darwinian? *Psychological Inquiry, 10*: 309–328.

Simonton, D. K. (2007). Specialised expertise or general cognitive processes? In M. J. Roberts (ed.), *Integrating the Mind: Domain General versus Domain Specific Processes in Higher Cognition* (p. 351). East Sussex: Psychology Press.

Simonton, D. K. (2009). Varieties of (scientific) creativity: A hierarchical model of domain-specific disposition, development, and achievement. *Perspectives on Psychological Science, 4*: 441–452.

Simonton, D. K. (2010). So you want to become a creative genius? You must be crazy! In D. Cropley, J. Kaufmann, A. Cropley, & M. Runco (eds.), *The Dark Side of Creativity* (pp. 218–234). New York: Cambridge University Press.

Sternberg, R. J. (1985). Implicit theories of intelligence, creativity, and wisdom. *Journal of Personality and Social Psychology, 49*: 607–627.

Sternberg, R. J. (2005). The domain generality versus specificity debate: How should it be posed? In J. C. Kaufman & J. Baer (eds.), *Creativity Across Domains: Faces of the Muse* (pp. 299–306). Hillsdale, NJ: Lawrence Erlbaum Associates.

Taylor, C. L. (2017). Creativity and mood disorder: A systematic review and meta-analysis. *Perspectives on Psychological Science, 12*(6): 1040–1076.

Taylor, C. L. & Kaufman, J. C. (2021). Values across creative domains. *The Journal of Creative Behavior, 55*: 501–516.

Taylor, C. L., McKay, A. S., & Kaufman, J. C. (2017). Creativity and personality: Nuances of domain and mood. In G. J. Feist, R. Reiter-Palmon, & J. C. Kaufman, *The Cambridge Handbook of Creativity and Personality Research* (pp. 167–186). New York: Cambridge University Press.

Thayer, L. (2021). The gut and brain, inextricably linked. Association for Psychological Science *Observer*, March/April 2021. www.psychological science.org/observer/gut-brain

Wallach, M. A. (1970). Creativity. In Mussen, P. H. (ed.), *Carmichael's Manual of Child Psychology, vol. 1* (pp. 1211–1272). Hoboken, NJ: Wiley.

Wallach, M. A. (1976). Tests tell us little about talent: Although measures of academic skills are widely used to determine access to contested educational opportunities, especially in their upper ranges they lack utility for predicting professional achievement. *American Scientist, 64*(1): 57–63.

Weinstein, E. C., Clark, Z., DiBartlomomeo, D. J., & Davis, K. (2014). A decline in creativity? It depends on the domain. *Creativity Research Journal, 26*: 174–184.

Wittgenstein, L. (1953). *Philosophical Investigations*. Oxford: Basil & Blackwell.

Wittgenstein, L. (1965). *Generally Known as the Blue and Brown Books: Preliminary Studies for the Philosophical Investigations*. New York: Harper & Row.

Cambridge Elements ≡

Creativity and Imagination

Anna Abraham
University of Georgia, USA

Anna Abraham, Ph.D. is the E. Paul Torrance Professor at the University of Georgia, USA. Her notable publications include *The Neuroscience of Creativity* (2018, Cambridge University Press) and the edited volume, *The Cambridge Handbook of the Imagination* (2020).

About the Series
Cambridge Elements in Creativity and Imagination publishes original perspectives and insightful reviews of empirical research, methods, theories, or applications in the vast fields of creativity and the imagination. The series is particularly focused on showcasing novel, necessary and neglected perspectives.

Cambridge Elements ☰

Creativity and Imagination

Elements in the Series

Printed in the United States
by Baker & Taylor Publisher Services